Whole Grain Recipes

Jean Paré

www.companyscoming.com
visit our website

Front Cover

1. Spinach Rice Salad, page 59

Props courtesy of: Chintz & Company

Back Cover

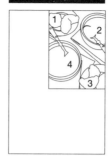

1. Chai, Millet and Rice Biscuits, page 46
2. Spicy Coconut Rice Soup, page 62
3. Savoury Drop Biscuits, page 52
4. Avocado Rice Soup, page 65

Props courtesy of: Pier 1 Imports
Stokes
Canadian Tire
Danesco Inc.
Pfaltzgraff Cana

Whole Grain Recipes

Copyright © Company's Coming Publishing Limited

First Printing May 2011

Library and Archives Canada Cataloguing in Publication
Paré, Jean, date-
Whole grain recipes / Jean Paré.
(Original series) Includes index.
At head of title: Company's Coming.
ISBN 978-1-897477-32-8
1. Healthy cooking (Cookery) I. Title. II. Series:
Paré, Jean, date-. Original series.
TX740.P37 2008   641.8'1   C2007-905155-3

We gratefully acknowledge the following suppliers for their generous support of our Test and Photography Kitchens:

Broil King Barbecues
Corelle®
Hamilton Beach® Canada
Lagostina®
Proctor Silex® Canada
Tupperware®

Published by
Company's Coming Publishing Limited
2311 – 96 Street
Edmonton, Alberta, Canada T6N 1G3
Tel: 780-450-6223   Fax: 780-450-1857
www.companyscoming.com

Company's Coming is a registered trademark owned by Company's Coming Publishing Limited

We acknowledge the financial support of the Government of Canada through the Canada Book Fund for our publishing activities.

Printed in China

Get more great recipes...FREE!

click

search

print

cook

From apple pie to zucchini bread, we've got you covered. Browse our free online recipes for Guaranteed Great!™ results.

You can also sign up to receive our **FREE online newsletter**. You'll receive exclusive offers, FREE recipes & cooking tips, new title previews, and much more…all delivered to your in-box.

So don't delay, visit our website today!

www.companyscoming.com
visit our ✦ website

Company's Coming Cookbooks

Quick & easy recipes; everyday ingredients!

2-in-1 Cookbook Collection

- Softcover, 256 pages
- Lay-flat plastic coil binding
- Full-colour photos
- Nutrition information

Original Series

- Softcover, 160 pages
- Lay-flat plastic comb binding
- Full-colour photos
- Updated format

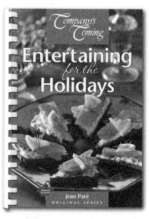

Special Occasion Series

- Softcover, 176 pages
- Full-colour photos
- Nutrition information

Original Series

- Softcover, 160 pages
- Lay-flat plastic comb binding
- Full-colour photos
- Nutrition information

For a complete listing of our cookbooks, visit our website:
www.companyscoming.com

Table of Contents

Appetizers

Breakfasts

Breads

Salads

Soups

Sides

Entrees

Desserts

Snacks

The Company's Coming Story

Jean Paré (pronounced "jeen PAIR-ee") grew up understanding that the combination of family, friends and home cooking is the best recipe for a good life. From her mother, she learned to appreciate good cooking, while her father praised even her earliest attempts in the kitchen. When Jean left home, she took with her a love of cooking, many family recipes and an intriguing desire to read cookbooks as if they were novels!

"Never share a recipe you wouldn't use yourself."

When her four children had all reached school age, Jean volunteered to cater the 50th anniversary celebration of the Vermilion School of Agriculture, now Lakeland College, in Alberta, Canada. Working out of her home, Jean prepared a dinner for more than 1,000 people, launching a flourishing catering operation that continued for over 18 years. During that time, she had countless opportunities to test new ideas with immediate feedback—resulting in empty plates and contented customers! Whether preparing cocktail sandwiches for a house party or serving a hot meal for 1,500 people, Jean Paré earned a reputation for great food, courteous service and reasonable prices.

As requests for her recipes increased, Jean was often asked the question, "Why don't you write a cookbook?" Jean responded by teaming up with her son, Grant Lovig, in the fall of 1980 to form Company's Coming Publishing Limited. The publication of *150 Delicious Squares* on April 14, 1981 marked the debut of what would soon become one of the world's most popular cookbook series.

The company has grown since those early days when Jean worked from a spare bedroom in her home. Today, she continues to write recipes while working closely with the staff of the Recipe Factory, as the Company's Coming test kitchen is affectionately known.

There she fills the role of mentor, assisting with the development of recipes people most want to use for everyday cooking and easy entertaining. Every Company's Coming recipe is *kitchen-tested* before it is approved for publication.

Jean's daughter, Gail Lovig, is responsible for marketing and distribution, leading a team that includes sales personnel located in major cities across Canada. Company's Coming cookbooks are distributed in Canada, the United States, Australia and other world markets. Bestsellers many times over in English, Company's Coming cookbooks have also been published in French and Spanish.

Familiar and trusted in home kitchens around the world, Company's Coming cookbooks are offered in a variety of formats. Highly regarded as kitchen workbooks, the softcover Original Series, with its lay-flat plastic comb binding, is still a favourite among readers.

Jean Paré's approach to cooking has always called for *quick and easy recipes* using *everyday ingredients.* That view has served her well. The recipient of many awards, including the Queen Elizabeth Golden Jubilee Medal, Jean was appointed Member of the Order of Canada, her country's highest lifetime achievement honour.

Jean continues to gain new supporters by adhering to what she calls The Golden Rule of Cooking: *Never share a recipe you wouldn't use yourself.* It's an approach that has worked—*millions of times over!*

Foreword

We live in a world of fad diets. Who knows how much paper has been used to promote all those here-today, gone-tomorrow eating choices? From the grapefruit diet to that oh-so-infamous cabbage-soup diet, there is no end to the eating regimens some so-called experts proclaim will get you into top shape in a matter of weeks.

Now that the 15 seconds of fame afforded to these fad diets has expired, experts are telling us that we should eat "smart carbs" and plenty of whole grains—but this is no fad. Good eating isn't about the diet-of-the-month, it's about making healthy choices for you and your family. By making some subtle changes to your family's menu, you can make the foods you already know and love just that much healthier. Using whole grains in your recipes is one key change you can make.

Why are whole grains important? Most of us who grew up on white bread know it is made from refined grains. Well, that refining process takes pretty well all of the B vitamins and Vitamin E from the grain, making it less nutritious. Unrefined whole grains are a much healthier alternative to refined flours and grains. The fibre in whole grains helps promote healthy digestion—and the type of

carbohydrate contained in whole grains is actually very healthy. As you will find out, many of the grains used in Whole Grain Recipes are packed with protein and a wide range of minerals.

I hope that with this book, I can show you just how delicious whole-grain foods can be. From hearty entrees like Everyday Baked Chicken to Stuffed Pork Tenderloin, desserts like Amaranth Baklava, to snacks such as Almond Buckwheat Brittle and Puffed Wheat Fruit Squares, this book will reveal to you the joys of whole-grain eating!

Jean Paré

Nutrition Information Guidelines

Each recipe is analyzed using the most current version of the Canadian Nutrient File from Health Canada, which is based on the United States Department of Agriculture (USDA) Nutrient Database.

- If more than one ingredient is listed (such as "butter or hard margarine"), or if a range is given (1 – 2 tsp., 5 – 10 mL), only the first ingredient or first amount is analyzed.

- For meat, poultry and fish, the serving size per person is based on the recommended 4 oz. (113 g) uncooked weight (without bone), which is 2 – 3 oz. (57 – 85 g) cooked weight (without bone)—approximately the size of a deck of playing cards.

- Milk used is 1% M.F. (milk fat), unless otherwise stated.

- Cooking oil used is canola oil, unless otherwise stated.

- Ingredients indicating "sprinkle," "optional," or "for garnish" are not included in the nutrition information.

- The fat in recipes and combination foods can vary greatly depending on the sources and types of fats used in each specific ingredient. For these reasons, the amount of saturated, monounsaturated and polyunsaturated fats may not add up to the total fat content.

Vera C. Mazurak, Ph.D.
Nutritionist

Your Grain Guide

The Eternal Struggle Between Good and Bad

A good diet balances all of the food groups. And considering grains make up one of the major food groups recognized by *Canada's Food Guide to Healthy Eating*, it's essential to include them in your family's meal plans.

The word "carbohydrate" now puts fear into a lot of people, thanks to the low-carb diet fad. But, good carbs are essential for a healthy diet. In fact, Health Canada recommends that people get 55 per cent of their food energy from carbohydrates. Believe it or not, before the low-carb craze, Health Canada studies showed that the average Canadian was getting just 48 per cent of his or her energy from good carbs. To maintain a healthy diet, we should have been increasing our intake of healthy carbs, not cutting them out!

So, what's the difference between a bad carb and a good carb? Bad carbs are essentially refined carbohydrates—like the sugars you find in soda pop and candy, or the refined grains you find in white rice and white flour. Some have almost no nutrient value, and the others have lost many of their nutrients in the refining process. And, worst of all, they taste good and are readily available, so many people tend to overindulge.

So, if bad carbs are refined, it would make sense that good carbs are unrefined. There are three main reasons why unrefined carbohydrates are good for you: they haven't lost any of their nutrients during the refining process; they take longer to break down, so your body can regulate them better and use them more efficiently; and they are full of fibre—meaning they keep you feeling full for longer, and they keep your digestive system operating effectively.

People sometimes forget that we are actually surrounded by good carbs. They're in dairy foods, fruits (no one would tell you to stop eating oranges and apples, right?), vegetables and, the topic of this book, whole grains. People may, at first, be a little wary of trying whole grains because they seem new and unfamiliar. It is true that whole grains may not be as convenient as refined grains—they take longer to cook and sometimes their availability may be limited—but good food and good eating take time. Of course it is easier to stop at the drive-thru, but consider making the effort to eat healthy as time well spent.

Cooking Grains *au Naturel*

Not all whole grains are equal. Some, like bulgur, have been partially processed before making their way to the market. Hard red wheat, on the other hand, is grain in its purest available form.

Using whole grains is not hard, but they usually require longer cooking times and may need to be pre-soaked before use—unless you are toasting them. And since amaranth may not take the same amount of time to cook as oats, we've made it easy for you—the instructions on how to prepare each grain are listed below.

AMARANTH

Water	1 3/4 cups	425 mL
Salt	1/8 tsp.	0.5 mL
Amaranth	1 cup	250 mL

Measure water and salt into small saucepan. Bring to a boil. Add amaranth. Stir. Reduce heat to medium-low. Simmer, covered, for about 25 minutes, without stirring, until liquid is absorbed and amaranth is tender. Makes about 2 cups (500 mL).

BUCKWHEAT

Water	2/3 cup	150 mL
Salt	1/8 tsp.	0.5 mL
Whole buckwheat	1/3 cup	75 mL

Measure water and salt into small saucepan. Bring to a boil. Add buckwheat. Stir. Reduce heat to medium-low. Simmer, covered, for about 15 minutes, without stirring, until liquid is absorbed and buckwheat is tender. Makes about 2/3 cup (150 mL).

For a larger yield of about 2 2/3 cups (650 mL), increase water to 1 1/2 cups (375 mL) and buckwheat to 1 cup (250 mL). Cook as directed.

BULGUR

Water	1 1/2 cups	375 mL
Salt	1/8 tsp.	0.5 mL
Bulgur	1 cup	250 mL

Measure water and salt into small saucepan. Bring to a boil. Add bulgur. Stir. Remove from heat. Let stand, covered, for about 30 minutes until liquid is absorbed and bulgur is tender. Makes about 3 3/4 cups (925 mL).

CRACKED WHEAT

Water	2 cups	500 mL
Salt	1/4 tsp.	1 mL
Cracked wheat	1 cup	250 mL

Measure water and salt into small saucepan. Bring to a boil. Add wheat. Stir. Reduce heat to medium-low. Simmer, uncovered, for about 12 minutes, without stirring, until wheat is tender. Drain. Makes about 2 1/2 cups (625 mL).

HARD RED WHEAT

Hard red wheat	1 cup	250 mL
Water, to cover		
Water	2 1/2 cups	625 mL
Salt	1/4 tsp.	1 mL

Measure wheat into small bowl. Cover with water. Let stand for at least 6 hours or overnight. Drain.

Measure second amount of water and salt into small saucepan. Bring to a boil. Add wheat. Stir. Reduce heat to medium-low. Simmer, covered, for about 1 3/4 hours, without stirring, until liquid is absorbed and wheat is tender. Makes about 2 1/2 cups (625 mL).

LARGE FLAKE ROLLED OATS

Water	2 1/2 cups	625 mL
Salt	1/8 tsp.	0.5 mL
Large flake rolled oats	1 cup	250 mL

Measure water and salt into small saucepan. Bring to a boil. Add oats. Stir. Remove from heat. Let stand, covered, for about 10 minutes until liquid is absorbed and oats are tender. Makes about 2 1/2 cups (625 mL).

LONG-GRAIN BROWN RICE

Water	2/3 cup	150 mL
Salt, sprinkle		
Long-grain brown rice	1/3 cup	75 mL

Measure water and salt into small saucepan. Bring to a boil. Add rice. Stir. Reduce heat to medium-low. Simmer, covered, for about 35 minutes, without stirring, until rice is tender. Remove from heat. Let stand, covered, for about 5 minutes until liquid is absorbed. Makes about 1 cup (250 mL).

For a larger yield of about 1 1/2 cups (375 mL), increase water to 1 cup (250 mL), salt to 1/8 tsp. (0.5 mL) and rice to 1/2 cup (125 mL). Cook as directed.

For a yield of about 2 cups (500 mL), increase water to 1 1/3 cups (325 mL), salt to 1/8 tsp. (0.5 mL) and rice to 2/3 cup (150 mL). Cook as directed.

MILLET

Water	3/4 cup	175 mL
Salt, sprinkle		
Millet	1/4 cup	60 mL

Measure water and salt into small saucepan. Bring to a boil. Add millet. Stir. Reduce heat to medium-low. Simmer, covered, for about 30 minutes, without stirring, until liquid is absorbed and millet is tender. Makes about 1 cup (250 mL).

Because the texture and taste of millet is slightly altered by freezing, try to make as close to the right volume of cooked millet as possible for your recipe. Frozen millet is fine for use in saucy recipes, but should not be used in salads.

For a yield of about 2 cups (500 mL), increase water to 1 1/4 cups (300 mL), salt to 1/8 tsp. (0.5 mL) and millet to 1/2 cup (125 mL). Cook as directed.

For a yield of about 3 cups (750 mL), increase water to 1 1/2 cups (375 mL), salt to 1/8 tsp. (0.5 mL) and millet to 3/4 cup (175 mL). Cook as directed.

POT BARLEY

Water	1 1/4 cup	300 mL
Salt	1/8 tsp.	0.5 mL
Pot barley	1/3 cup	75 mL

Measure water and salt into small saucepan. Bring to a boil. Add barley. Stir. Reduce heat to medium-low. Simmer, covered, for about 1 hour, without stirring, until liquid is absorbed and barley is tender. Makes about 1 1/2 cups (375 mL).

For a larger yield of about 3 3/4 cups (925 mL), use a medium saucepan, increase water to 3 cups (750 mL), salt to 3/4 tsp. (4 mL) and pot barley to 1 cup (250 mL). Cook as directed.

QUINOA

Water	1/2 cup	125 mL
Salt	1/8 tsp.	0.5 mL
Quinoa, rinsed and drained	1/3 cup	75 mL

Measure water and salt into small saucepan. Bring to a boil. Add quinoa. Stir. Reduce heat to medium-low. Simmer, covered, for about 20 minutes, without stirring, until liquid is absorbed and quinoa is tender. Makes about 1 cup (250 mL).

For a larger yield of about 1 1/2 cups (375 mL), increase water to 3/4 cup (175 mL) and quinoa to 1/2 cup (125 mL). Cook as directed.

WILD RICE

Water	1 1/2 cups	375 mL
Salt	1/8 tsp.	0.5 mL
Wild rice	1/2 cup	125 mL

Measure water and salt into small saucepan. Bring to a boil. Add wild rice. Stir. Reduce heat to medium-low. Simmer, covered, for about 75 minutes, without stirring, until wild rice is tender. Drain any remaining liquid. Makes about 1 1/2 cups (375 mL).

Because wild rice has a long cooking time, making larger volumes is more sensible. Wild rice freezes well, but becomes a bit moist.

For a yield of about 2 cups (500 mL), increase water to 2 cups (500 mL) and rice to 2/3 cup (150 mL). Cook as directed.

For a yield of about 3 cups (750 mL), increase water to 2 1/2 cups (625 mL), salt to 1/4 tsp. (1 mL) and rice to 1 cup (250 mL). Cook as directed.

For a yield of about 4 cups (1 L) use a medium saucepan, increase water to 3 cups (750 mL), salt to 1/4 tsp. (1 mL) and rice to 1 1/2 cups (375 mL). Cook as directed.

Gathering Your Grains

Grains are hardy, but that doesn't mean they can't spoil. Whole grains contain the germ of the grain, which can go bad over time. So, to make sure your uncooked grains stay as fresh as possible for as long as possible, make sure they're kept in a cool place—the freezer is ideal—in tight storage containers. The container is the key: it must be tightly sealed because any moisture that gets into the grain will speed up the spoiling process.

You can't think about storing whole grains like you would refined white flour. The refining process may strip the grain of nutrients, but it also takes out the parts of the grain that can spoil. Comparing whole grains to refined grains is like comparing geese to gooseberries!

Some whole grains are partially cooked or processed before making their way to your kitchen—bulgur is the best example. But, even if the germ has been removed, think of whole grains as you would meat, fruit or vegetables. They are all perishable.

Once grains have been cooked, they do have some staying power. Usually, they can be reheated or used in other recipes safely for about a week, as long as they are stored in a tightly sealed container. Of course, you can cook a large batch and freeze it for a longer period of time. Just portion the cooked grains into smaller containers so you don't have to thaw out a lot when all you need is a little!

Mixing It Up: Grain Blends

In this section, we've compiled a list of various multi-purpose grain blends. Some are used in other recipes in the book and some of them are great as stand-alone side dishes or breakfasts.

WILD AND WHITE RICE BLEND

Don't want your side dish to overshadow your entree? This simple blend is unique enough not to be boring, but simple enough to blend well with the rest of your meal.

Water	2 1/2 cups	625 mL
Salt	1/4 tsp.	1 mL
Wild rice	1/3 cup	75 mL
Long-grain white rice	3/4 cup	175 mL

Combine water and salt in medium saucepan. Bring to a boil. Add wild rice. Stir. Reduce heat to medium-low. Simmer, covered, for 45 minutes, without stirring. Bring to a boil.

Add white rice. Stir. Reduce heat to medium-low. Simmer, covered, for about 20 minutes, without stirring, until rice is tender and liquid is absorbed. Makes about 3 1/3 cups (825 mL).

1 cup (250 mL): 230 Calories; 0.6 g Total Fat (0.1 g Mono, 0.2 g Poly, 0.1 g Sat); 0 mg Cholesterol; 50 g Carbohydrate; 2 g Fibre; 6 g Protein; 179 mg Sodium

WILD AND BROWN RICE BLEND

Another easy side that showcases the flavours of your meal.

Water	2 1/2 cups	625 mL
Salt	1/4 tsp.	1 mL
Wild rice	1/2 cup	125 mL
Long-grain brown rice	1/2 cup	125 mL

Combine water and salt in medium saucepan. Bring to a boil. Add wild rice. Stir. Reduce heat to medium-low. Simmer, covered, for 30 minutes, without stirring. Bring to a boil.

Add brown rice. Stir. Reduce heat to medium-low. Simmer, covered, for 25 to 30 minutes, without stirring, until rice is tender and liquid is absorbed. Makes about 3 1/2 cups (875 mL).

1 cup (250 mL): 190 Calories; 1.1 g Total Fat (0.3 g Mono, 0.5 g Poly, 0.2 g Sat); 0 mg Cholesterol; 40 g Carbohydrate; 3 g Fibre; 6 g Protein; 174 mg Sodium

ALL-PURPOSE COATING

Consider this your go-to recipe when you simply want to shake, then bake, your meat.

Crushed whole-wheat squares cereal	1 cup	250 mL
Whole-wheat flour	3/4 cup	175 mL
Ground almonds	1/4 cup	60 mL
Yellow cornmeal	1/4 cup	60 mL
Brown sugar, packed	1 tbsp.	15 mL
Paprika	1 tbsp.	15 mL
Onion powder	2 tsp.	10 mL
Seasoned salt	2 tsp.	10 mL
Garlic powder	1 tsp.	5 mL
Pepper	1 tsp.	5 mL
Poultry seasoning	1 tsp.	5 mL
Cayenne pepper	1/2 tsp.	2 mL
Olive oil	1 tbsp.	15 mL

Combine first 12 ingredients in medium bowl.

Drizzle with olive oil. Stir well. Store in refrigerator for up to 1 week or in the freezer for up to 2 months. Makes about 2 1/2 cups (625 mL).

1 tbsp. (15 mL): 23 Calories; 0.7 g Total Fat (0.4 g Mono, 0.1 g Poly, 0.1 g Sat); 0 mg Cholesterol; 4 g Carbohydrate; 1 g Fibre; 1 g Protein; 67 mg Sodium

CHICKEN WITH ALL-PURPOSE COATING: Measure 3/4 cup (175 mL) All-Purpose Coating into small shallow bowl. Spray cooking spray on both sides of 6 boneless, skinless chicken breast halves (4 – 6 oz., 113 – 140 g, each). Press both sides of chicken into coating mixture until coated. Arrange on greased baking sheet with sides. Spray chicken with cooking spray. Bake in 375°F (190°C) oven for 30 to 45 minutes, turning every 15 minutes, until crispy and internal temperature reaches 170°F (77°C).

PORK WITH ALL-PURPOSE COATING: Measure 3/4 cup (175 mL) All-Purpose Coating into small shallow bowl. Spray cooking spray on both sides of 6 pork chops. Press both sides of pork into coating mixture until coated. Arrange on greased baking sheet with sides. Spray pork with cooking spray. Bake in 375°F (190°C) oven for about 20 minutes, turning at halftime, until crispy and internal temperature reaches 160°F (71°C).

FISH WITH ALL-PURPOSE COATING: Measure 3/4 cup (175 mL) All-Purpose Coating into small shallow bowl. Spray cooking spray on both sides of 6 fresh (or frozen, thawed) haddock fillets (or other firm white fish). Press both sides of fish into coating mixture until coated. Arrange on greased baking sheet with sides. Spray fish with cooking spray. Bake in 375°F (190°C) oven for about 15 minutes, turning at halftime, until crispy and fish flakes easily when tested with a fork.

WHOLE-GRAIN CEREAL BLEND

Makes a delicious, multi-textured hot cereal. If you find the quinoa slightly bitter, add brown sugar or your favourite sweetener.

Hard red wheat	1/2 cup	125 mL
Whole buckwheat	1/2 cup	125 mL
Millet	1/4 cup	60 mL
Quinoa (see Note)	1/4 cup	60 mL
Long-grain brown rice	2 tbsp.	30 mL
Large flake rolled oats	1/2 cup	125 mL

Process first 5 ingredients in food processor or blender for about 1 minute until coarsely ground.

Add oats. Stir. Makes about 2 cups (500 mL).

1/4 cup (60 mL): 174 Calories; 1.7 g Total Fat (0.4 g Mono, 0.7 g Poly, 0.3 g Sat); 0 mg Cholesterol; 34 g Carbohydrate; 4 g Fibre; 6 g Protein; 4 mg Sodium

Note: Quinoa must not be rinsed in this recipe because it is mixed with other dry grains.

HOT WHOLE-GRAIN CEREAL: Combine 2 1/2 cups (625 mL) water and 1/4 tsp. (1 mL) salt in medium saucepan. Bring to a boil. Add 1 cup (250 mL) Whole-Grain Cereal Blend. Stir. Reduce heat to medium-low. Simmer, covered, for about 10 minutes, stirring occasionally, until oats are tender. Makes about 2 1/3 cups (575 mL).

Getting to Know You

So, never heard of some of these grains? Wonder what they're all about? Here's a primer on some of the grains you can find at your local market or health-food store.

Amaranth — It's a plant that has been the subject of famous English poems and inspired the name of an Ontario township. Native to South America, it was worshipped by Aztecs as its seeds were rumoured to provide magical powers to anyone who ate them. Maybe the Aztecs knew just how good a source of iron amaranth seeds are! Today, amaranth can provide magic to your dishes. Friendly for gluten-free diets, amaranth seeds and flour are growing in popularity. The seeds can be combined with other grains in baking or can be used on their own as a healthy cereal!

Brown rice — Brown rice is simply the unrefined version of the white rice you see on the grocery store shelves. The rice grains are brown when they are removed from the hull, and can be cooked as is. But, many food producers choose to polish the rice so it becomes white. This process robs the rice of many nutrients, including most of its B vitamins and iron.

Buckwheat — We have all eaten buckwheat pancakes at some time or another, but did you know buckwheat is a versatile plant that has been used by the Chinese in their everyday cooking for centuries? The Canadian Grain Commission points out that buckwheat is not a cereal and is not at all related to wheat—but it can be milled into a flour that can be used in the same recipes as wheat flour. Buckwheat has plenty of Vitamin E and flavinoids, which have been rumoured to be cancer-fighting nutrients. Rutin, a buckwheat extract, is used to treat patients with high blood pressure.

Bulgur — Bulgur is famous in Middle Eastern cuisine. It puffs up when cooked, and is used as a side dish or as an ingredient in stews and soups. Bulgur is whole wheat that has been sifted after being cracked, parboiled (partially cooked) and dried. These boiling and drying processes make bulgur easier to cook or to use in baking, as it doesn't need to be pre-soaked like some other whole grains. Because it hasn't been refined, it keeps its full nutritional value. Bulgur is low in fat and high in calcium and phosphorus. It's also an excellent source of antioxidants.

Cracked wheat — It's easy to tell the difference between bulgur and cracked wheat. With bulgur, the wheat berry is semi-cooked after it has been broken. Cracked wheat will not be cooked before being put onto the shelves at the market. It is exactly what its name indicates—raw, cracked wheat berries. The difference: in the bulgur sifting process, some bran may be removed. With cracked wheat, you get all the fibre of the bran.

1. Amaranth
2. Brown Rice
3. Buckwheat
4. Bulgur
5. Cracked Wheat
6. Millet

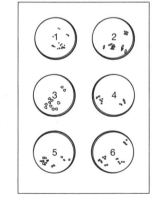

16

Millet — Millet has been used in baking by the Chinese for thousands of years. It's popular in India, where it's used to make flatbread, and people around the world also use these tiny grains to make beer. In North America, it has traditionally been thought of as a grain meant for animal feed. But those times are changing, and its use as a whole grain for the kitchen is increasing. Millet is gluten-free and is packed with B vitamins and protein. It's also the easiest of all grains to digest. And we thought it was just for cows!

Oat flakes — Next to wheat, this is the grain most recognized by North American shoppers. We've all had oatmeal or toasted-oat cereal, haven't we? Oats are cereal grains that are grown across Canada and the United States. Oats, which used to be called "havers" by English and Scottish farmers, are high in fibre and protein. At one time, they were considered a common grain because they were cheaper to grow and cost less on the market than wheat.

Pot barley — Also known as Scotch barley, "pot" is the term for barley that has been hulled. Until it's been hulled, barley is pretty well inedible—no matter what you do to it. But, once it's reached the pot barley stage, it's a grain that is packed with food energy. Barley has more than twice the riboflavin of wheat and is a great source of vitamin E. Barley puffs up when boiled in water, which makes it great for soups. Barley flour can also be used as a wheat flour substitute.

Quinoa — Quinoa (pronounced KEEN-wah) is so durable a plant, and offers such nutritious seeds, that the United Nations calls it a "supercrop" and is funding growing projects around the world. The Incans called quinoa the "Mother Grain" and, as the name implies, it has been a staple in South American civilizations for thousands of years. Because the plant can survive cold weather and harsh soil conditions, it is a perfect crop for civilizations living in the Andes. It boasts a high protein content as well as the full range of amino acids. The leaves can also be eaten, though it's the seeds that are used in cooking and baking. Unless you are using quinoa dry, it should be rinsed in a fine-mesh sieve to get rid of its bitter coating.

Wheat berries — This is simply the term that's used for the grains directly harvested from the wheat fields. These nuggets can be sent to market as is, ground into flour or refined. Wheat berries are the starting point for both bulgur and cracked wheat. To get all the nutrients possible from wheat, including its high fibre and protein content, you can use this form of wheat in your cooking or baking. The variety of wheat berry we use in this book is hard red wheat.

Wild rice — There is a Chinese variety of wild rice, but that's not to be confused with this nutritious grass that can be found in wetlands across its native North America. Although not technically a grain, it is usually grouped in the grain category because of its nutritional similarity to grains. North American aboriginals used to harvest it right from their canoes, and it's an official symbol of the State of Minnesota. It's high in protein, low in fat, and is suitable for gluten-free diets.

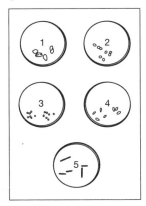

1. Oat Flakes
2. Pot Barley
3. Quinoa
4. Wheat Berries
5. Wild Rice

19

Cracked Wheat Dolmades

These cracked wheat, pine nut and raisin-stuffed grape leaves are sure to grab everyone's attention.

Olive oil	2 tsp.	10 mL
Chopped onion	1 cup	250 mL
Garlic clove, minced	1	1
(or 1/4 tsp., 1 mL, powder)		
Cracked wheat	3/4 cup	175 mL
Chopped pine nuts	1/2 cup	125 mL
Prepared chicken broth	1/2 cup	125 mL
Raisins	1/2 cup	125 mL
Chopped fresh dill	3 tbsp.	50 mL
(or 2 1/4 tsp., 11 mL, dried)		
Chopped fresh parsley	3 tbsp.	50 mL
(or 2 1/4 tsp., 11 mL, flakes)		
Chopped fresh mint	2 tbsp.	30 mL
(or 1 1/2 tsp., 7 mL, dried)		
Grape leaves, rinsed and drained, tough stems removed (see Note)	8	8
Grape leaves, rinsed and drained, tough stems removed (see Note)	25	25
Lemon juice	1 1/2 tbsp.	25 mL
Olive oil	2 tbsp.	30 mL
Grape leaves, rinsed and drained, tough stems removed (see Note)	7	7
Prepared chicken broth	1/2 cup	125 mL
Water	1/2 cup	125 mL

Heat first amount of olive oil in small frying pan on medium. Add onion and garlic. Cook for about 5 minutes, stirring often, until onion starts to soften. Remove from heat.

Add next 7 ingredients. Stir. Set aside.

Cover bottom and sides of greased 2 quart (2 L) casserole with first amount of grape leaves.

(continued on next page)

Place second amount of grape leaves on work surface, vein-side up, stem-end (bottom of leaf) closest to you. Place about 1 tbsp. (15 mL) wheat mixture about 1/2 inch (12 mm) from bottom of leaf. Fold bottom of leaf over wheat mixture. Fold in sides. Roll up from bottom to enclose filling. Repeat with remaining leaves and wheat mixture. Arrange rolls, seam-side down, close together over leaves in casserole.

Sprinkle with lemon juice and second amount of olive oil. Cover rolls with third amount of grape leaves.

Add second amount of broth and water. Bake, covered, in 350°F (175°C) oven for about 30 minutes until wheat is tender. Makes 25 dolmades.

1 dolmade: 67 Calories; 3.3 g Total Fat (1.7 g Mono, 0.9 g Poly, 0.5 g Sat); 0 mg Cholesterol; 8 g Carbohydrate; 1 g Fibre; 2 g Protein; 215 mg Sodium

Pictured on page 35.

Note: Grape leaves can generally be found in the import section of your grocery store.

Paré Pointer

Little Johnny didn't lose his two front teeth. He had them in his pocket.

Couscous-Stuffed Peppers

Anchors away! Set sail for great taste with red pepper boats loaded with a delicious cargo of couscous, bacon and tomato.

Prepared chicken broth	3/4 cup	250 mL
Ground coriander	1/4 tsp.	1 mL
Ground cumin	1/4 tsp.	1 mL
Bulgur	1/4 cup	60 mL
Whole-wheat couscous	1/4 cup	60 mL
Bacon slices, diced	2	2
Chopped celery	1/4 cup	60 mL
Chopped onion	1/4 cup	60 mL
Small garlic clove, minced (or 1/8 tsp., 0.5 mL, powder)	1	1
Large egg, fork-beaten	1	1
Diced tomato	1/2 cup	125 mL
Diced green pepper	1/4 cup	60 mL
Salt, sprinkle		
Pepper, sprinkle		
Large red (or green) peppers, quartered lengthwise	2	2
Prepared chicken broth	1/4 cup	60 mL
Grated jalapeño Monterey Jack cheese	1/2 cup	125 mL

Combine first 3 ingredients in medium saucepan. Bring to a boil. Add bulgur and couscous. Stir. Remove from heat. Let stand, covered, for about 10 minutes until liquid is absorbed. Fluff with fork.

Cook bacon in medium frying pan on medium until almost crisp. Drain all but 1 tsp. (5 mL) drippings.

Add next 3 ingredients. Cook for about 5 minutes, stirring often, until onion is softened and bacon is crisp. Add to couscous mixture. Stir.

Combine next 5 ingredients in medium bowl. Add couscous mixture. Stir.

Cut quartered red peppers in half crosswise. Spoon couscous mixture into red pepper pieces.

(continued on next page)

Appetizers

Pour second amount of broth into greased 9 x 13 inch (22 x 33 cm) pan. Place stuffed peppers in broth. Cover with foil. Bake in 350°F (175°C) oven for 30 to 35 minutes until red pepper is tender-crisp. Remove and discard foil.

Sprinkle cheese over top. Bake, uncovered, for about 10 minutes until cheese is melted. Makes 16 stuffed peppers.

1 stuffed pepper: 50 Calories; 2.2 g Total Fat (0.8 g Mono, 0.2 g Poly, 1.0 g Sat); 16 mg Cholesterol; 5 g Carbohydrate; 1 g Fibre; 3 g Protein; 92 mg Sodium

Pictured on page 35.

Variation: To make stuffed peppers as a side dish, cut red peppers in half lengthwise instead of cutting into quarters and fill with the couscous mixture. Bake as directed.

Crisp Rye Rounds

Forget those fat-filled potato chips and store-bought crackers—these rounds have all the flavour and none of the guilt. Great on their own, or try them with hummus or a creamy, low-fat dip.

All-purpose flour	1 1/2 cups	375 mL
Rye flour	1 cup	250 mL
Brown sugar, packed	2 tbsp.	30 mL
Baking powder	1 tsp.	5 mL
Ground cardamom	1/2 tsp.	2 mL
Salt	1/4 tsp.	1 mL
Cold butter (or hard margarine), cut up	1/4 cup	60 mL
Water	1/2 cup	125 mL

Combine first 6 ingredients in large bowl. Cut in butter until mixture resembles coarse crumbs.

Add water. Stir until soft dough forms. Turn out onto lightly floured surface. Knead 8 to 10 times until smooth. Divide into 6 equal portions. Roll portions into 8 inch (20 cm) diameter circles. Using your finger, make a 1 inch (2.5 cm) hole in centre of each circle to ensure even cooking. Prick entire surface of dough with fork through to bottom. Transfer circles to greased baking sheets. Bake in 325°F (160°C) oven for 15 minutes. Turn circles over. Bake for another 7 minutes until crisp. Remove circles from baking sheets and place on wire racks to cool. Break circles into pieces. Serves 12.

1 serving: 130 Calories; 4.1 g Total Fat (1.0 g Mono, 0.3 g Poly, 2.4 g Sat); 10 mg Cholesterol; 21 g Carbohydrate; 2 g Fibre; 2 g Protein; 99 mg Sodium

Buckwheat Shrimp Crostini

We've bucked convention and added a little buckwheat to this spicy, toasty crostini.
Use a whole-wheat or multi-grain baguette to up the whole-grain factor.

Baguette bread slices (1/2 inch, 12 mm, thick)	24	24
Olive (or canola) oil	2 tbsp.	30 mL
TOPPING		
Water	1/2 cup	125 mL
Salt, sprinkle		
Whole buckwheat	1/3 cup	75 mL
Butter (or hard margarine)	1 tbsp.	15 mL
Garlic cloves, minced (or 1/2 tsp., 2 mL, powder)	2	2
Lemon juice	1 tbsp.	15 mL
Paprika	1 tsp.	5 mL
Seasoned salt	1/2 tsp.	2 mL
Cayenne pepper	1/4 tsp.	1 mL
Chopped tomato	1 cup	250 mL
Frozen, uncooked shrimp (peeled and deveined), chopped	7 oz.	200 g
Chopped fresh parsley (or 3/4 tsp., 4 mL, flakes)	1 tbsp.	15 mL

Lightly brush bread slices with olive oil. Place on ungreased baking sheet with sides. Bake in 375°F (190°C) oven for about 15 minutes until golden and crisp. Let stand on baking sheet until cool enough to handle. Transfer to serving platter.

Topping: Combine water and salt in small saucepan. Bring to a boil. Add buckwheat. Stir. Reduce heat to medium-low. Simmer, covered, for about 15 minutes, without stirring, until buckwheat is tender and liquid is absorbed. Fluff with fork. Set aside.

Melt butter in large frying pan on medium-high. Add garlic. Heat and stir for 1 to 2 minutes until fragrant. Add next 4 ingredients. Stir.

Add remaining 3 ingredients. Heat and stir for 2 to 3 minutes until shrimp turn pink. Add buckwheat. Heat and stir for 2 to 3 minutes until heated through. Transfer to serving bowl. Serve on toasted bread slices. Makes 24 crostini.

(continued on next page)

Appetizers

1 baguette slice with 1 1/2 tbsp. (25 mL) topping: 105 Calories; 1.8 g Total Fat (1.0 g Mono, 0.2 g Poly, 0.5 g Sat); 14 mg Cholesterol; 17 g Carbohydrate; trace Fibre; 4 g Protein; 230 mg Sodium

Pictured on page 35.

Chewy Wheat Hummus

Is your hummus humdrum? Punch it up with the pleasing texture of whole wheat, then add pizzazz with a colourful tomato, olive and onion topping.

Water	1 cup	250 mL
Salt	1/8 tsp.	0.5 mL
Cracked wheat	1/2 cup	125 mL
Can of chickpeas (garbanzo beans), rinsed and drained	19 oz.	540 mL
Lemon juice	1/4 cup	60 mL
Water	1/4 cup	60 mL
Tahini (sesame paste)	3 tbsp.	50 mL
Garlic clove, halved	1	1
Grated lemon zest	1/2 tsp.	2 mL
Salt	1/4 tsp.	1 mL
TOPPING		
Diced seeded tomato	1/2 cup	125 mL
Finely chopped black olives	2 tbsp.	30 mL
Finely chopped red onion	2 tbsp.	30 mL
Olive oil	2 tsp.	10 mL

Combine water and salt in small saucepan. Bring to a boil. Add wheat. Stir. Reduce heat to medium-low. Simmer, uncovered, for about 12 minutes, without stirring, until wheat is tender. Drain.

Process next 7 ingredients in blender for about 1 minute until smooth. Add wheat. Process for about 30 seconds until smooth. Spread evenly on plate or in shallow serving dish.

Topping: Combine all 4 ingredients in small bowl. Spoon over chickpea mixture. Serve at room temperature. Makes about 3 1/4 cups (800 mL).

1/4 cup (60 mL): 118 Calories; 3.7 g Total Fat (1.5 g Mono, 1.3 g Poly, 0.5 g Sat); 0 mg Cholesterol; 17 g Carbohydrate; 3 g Fibre; 5 g Protein; 173 mg Sodium

Savoury Biscotti

Beam me up, biscotti! These crisp, spicy cookies are guaranteed to transport you out of this world.

All-purpose flour	1 cup	250 mL
Whole-wheat flour	1 cup	250 mL
Grated Parmesan cheese	3/4 cup	175 mL
Chopped pine nuts	1/2 cup	125 mL
Yellow cornmeal	1/4 cup	60 mL
Caraway seed	2 tsp.	10 mL
Baking powder	1 1/4 tsp.	6 mL
Baking soda	1/2 tsp.	2 mL
Lemon pepper	1/2 tsp.	2 mL
Salt	1/2 tsp.	2 mL
Coarsely ground pepper	1 tsp.	5 mL
Large eggs, fork-beaten	2	2
Buttermilk (or soured milk, see Tip, page 38)	1/2 cup	125 mL

Measure first 11 ingredients into large bowl. Stir. Make a well in centre.

Add eggs and buttermilk to well. Mix until stiff dough forms. Turn out onto lightly floured surface. Knead 6 times. Divide dough in half. Shape each half into 8 inch (20 cm) long log. Place logs crosswise on greased baking sheet, about 3 inches (7.5 cm) apart. Flatten logs slightly. Bake in 350°F (175°C) oven for about 30 minutes until golden. Let stand on baking sheet for about 20 minutes until cool enough to handle. Using serrated knife, cut logs diagonally into 1/2 inch (12 mm) slices. Arrange, evenly spaced apart, on greased baking sheet. Bake for about 20 minutes, turning at halftime, until dry and browned on bottom. Let stand on baking sheet for 5 minutes. Remove biscotti from baking sheet and place on wire racks to cool. Makes about 26 biscotti.

1 biscotti: 77 Calories; 3.0 g Total Fat (1.1 g Mono, 0.8 g Poly, 1.0 g Sat); 17 mg Cholesterol; 9 g Carbohydrate; 1 g Fibre; 4 g Protein; 148 mg Sodium

Eggplant Bulgur Spread

This tahini, garlic and lemon-flavoured spread is sure to spice things up at your next get-together. Serve with pita bread wedges or crackers.

Bulgur	1/3 cup	75 mL
Salt, just a pinch		
Boiling water	1/2 cup	125 mL
Cubed peeled eggplant	4 cups	1 L
Salt	1/2 tsp.	2 mL
Finely diced red pepper	1/2 cup	125 mL
Prepared vegetable broth	1/4 cup	60 mL
Plain yogurt	2 tbsp.	30 mL
Finely chopped green onion	1 tbsp.	15 mL
Lemon juice	1 tbsp.	15 mL
Olive oil	1 tbsp.	15 mL
Tahini (sesame paste)	1 tbsp.	15 mL
Chopped fresh cilantro or parsley	2 tsp.	10 mL
Garlic clove, minced	1	1
(or 1/4 tsp., 1 mL, powder)		
Ground cumin	1/4 tsp.	1 mL
Salt	1/4 tsp.	1 mL
Pepper	1/4 tsp.	1 mL

Combine bulgur and salt in small heatproof bowl. Add boiling water. Stir. Let stand, covered, for 30 minutes.

Arrange eggplant on greased baking sheet with sides. Sprinkle with salt. Bake in 400°F (205°C) oven for about 20 minutes until lightly browned and tender. Transfer to blender or food processor. Add bulgur. Process until almost smooth.

Add remaining 12 ingredients. Process until smooth. Makes about 2 cups (500 mL).

1/4 cup (60 mL): 58 Calories; 2.9 g Total Fat (1.6 g Mono, 0.6 g Poly, 0.5 g Sat); trace Cholesterol; 8 g Carbohydrate; 2 g Fibre; 2 g Protein; 263 mg Sodium

Salmon Quinoa Lettuce Cups

Ginger-flavoured salmon nestled in delicate lettuce leaves—we don't call
them appetizers for nothing.

Cooked quinoa (see page 11)	1 cup	250 mL
Can of skinless, boneless pink salmon, drained	6 oz.	170 g
Orange juice	1/4 cup	60 mL
Liquid honey	1 tbsp.	15 mL
Soy sauce	1 tsp.	5 mL
Dry mustard	1/2 tsp.	2 mL
Finely grated ginger root	1/2 tsp.	2 mL
Sesame oil (for flavour)	1/2 tsp.	2 mL
Small butter lettuce leaves	18	18
Sesame seeds, toasted (see Tip, below)	1 tbsp.	15 mL

Put quinoa and salmon into medium bowl. Toss.

Combine next 6 ingredients in small bowl. Add to quinoa mixture. Stir
until coated. Chill for about 1 hour until cold.

Arrange lettuce leaves in single layer on large serving platter. Place about
1 tbsp. (15 mL) quinoa mixture in centre of each leaf.

Sprinkle with sesame seeds. Makes 18 lettuce cups.

1 lettuce cup: 58 Calories; 1.3 g Total Fat (0.3 g Mono, 0.4 g Poly, 0.1 g Sat); 7 mg Cholesterol;
8 g Carbohydrate; 1 g Fibre; 4 g Protein; 64 mg Sodium

Pictured on page 35.

 tip   When toasting nuts, seeds or coconut, cooking times will vary
for each type of nut—so never toast them together. For small
amounts, place ingredient in an ungreased shallow frying pan.
Heat on medium for 3 to 5 minutes, stirring often, until golden.
For larger amounts, spread ingredient evenly in an ungreased
shallow pan. Bake in a 350°F (175°C) oven for 5 to 10 minutes,
stirring or shaking often, until golden.

Kutya

Kutya, a cold porridge, is traditionally served at Ukranian Christmas Eve dinner. It is meant to represent an abundant life—but it also makes one heck of a healthy breakfast. The preparation is a tad involved, but it will keep in the fridge for 10 days, or may be frozen for longer.

Hard red wheat	2 cups	500 mL
Water	8 cups	2 L
Water	5 1/2 cups	1.4 L
Salt	1 tsp.	5 mL
Poppy seeds	1/2 cup	125 mL
Water	1 cup	250 mL
Liquid honey	1/3 cup	75 mL
Chopped walnuts, toasted (see Tip, page 28), optional	1/2 cup	125 mL

Measure wheat into large bowl. Add water. Let stand, covered, for at least 8 hours. Drain. Transfer to 3 1/2 quart (3.5 L) slow cooker.

Add second amount of water and salt. Stir. Cook, covered, on Low for 7 to 8 hours or on High for 3 1/2 to 4 hours. Wheat should be split open and liquid should be thick and creamy. Drain, reserving 1 cup (250 mL) cooking water. Set aside.

Combine poppy seeds and water in small saucepan. Bring to a boil. Reduce heat to medium. Boil gently, uncovered, for 10 minutes. Drain through fine sieve. Transfer poppy seeds to blender.

Add honey. Process for about 1 minute until poppy seeds are ground. Add to wheat. Stir, adding reserved cooking water a little at a time until desired consistency.

Add walnuts. Stir. Serve at room temperature or chill until cold. Makes about 6 cups (1.5 L).

1 cup (250 mL): 393 Calories; 12.8 g Total Fat (1.8 g Mono, 8.7 g Poly, 1.4 g Sat); 0 mg Cholesterol; 62 g Carbohydrate; 10 g Fibre; 13 g Protein; 83 mg Sodium

Chai-Spiced Oatmeal

Would you like a little tea with your oatmeal? How about in your oatmeal? Join the legion of chai fanatics and see what all the fuss is about.

Water	3/4 cup	175 mL
Sweetened chai tea concentrate	1/2 cup	125 mL
Large flake rolled oats	1/2 cup	125 mL
Salt, sprinkle		
Grated peeled cooking apple (such as McIntosh)	1/2 cup	125 mL
Raisins	2 tbsp.	30 mL

Combine water and tea concentrate in small saucepan. Bring to a boil. Add oats and salt. Stir. Reduce heat to medium-low. Simmer, uncovered, for about 8 minutes, stirring often, until liquid is almost absorbed. Remove from heat.

Add apple and raisins. Stir. Let stand, covered, for about 5 minutes until oats are tender and raisins are plump. Makes about 1 1/2 cups (375 mL).

1 cup (250 mL): 234 Calories; 2.1 g Total Fat (0.6 g Mono, 0.9 g Poly, 0.6 g Sat); 0 mg Cholesterol; 50 g Carbohydrate; 4 g Fibre; 5 g Protein; 10 mg Sodium

PBAJ Smoothie

Peanut butter, amaranth and jam would be good in a sandwich, but are splendid in a smoothie.

Amaranth, toasted (see Tip, page 31)	3 tbsp.	50 mL
Milk	1 cup	250 mL
Vanilla yogurt	1/2 cup	125 mL
Smooth peanut butter	1/4 cup	60 mL
Raspberry jam	3 tbsp.	50 mL

Put amaranth into blender. Process until finely ground.

Add remaining 4 ingredients. Process until smooth. Makes about 2 cups (500 mL).

1 cup (250 mL): 436 Calories; 19.8 g Total Fat (8.4 g Mono, 5.0 g Poly, 4.9 g Sat); 8 mg Cholesterol; 52 g Carbohydrate; 4 g Fibre; 17 g Protein; 104 mg Sodium

Fruited Muesli

Start the day off right with this a-muesli-ing maple blend of fruits, nuts and oats. Stores in an airtight container in the refrigerator for up to four days.

Apple juice	1/2 cup	125 mL
Water	1/2 cup	125 mL
Large flake rolled oats	1 cup	250 mL
Chopped unpeeled cooking apple (such as McIntosh)	2 cups	500 mL
Plain yogurt	2 cups	500 mL
Chopped dried apricot	1/2 cup	125 mL
Raisins	1/2 cup	125 mL
Ground flaxseed (see Tip, page 49)	1/4 cup	60 mL
Sliced natural almonds, toasted (see Tip, page 28)	1/4 cup	60 mL
Unsalted, roasted sunflower seeds	1/4 cup	60 mL
Maple (or maple-flavoured) syrup	3 tbsp.	50 mL
Grated orange zest	1 tsp.	5 mL
Ground cinnamon	1 tsp.	5 mL

Combine apple juice and water in medium saucepan. Bring to a boil. Remove from heat. Add oats. Stir. Transfer to medium bowl. Chill for 25 to 30 minutes until liquid is absorbed.

Add remaining 10 ingredients. Stir. Makes about 6 cups (1.5 L).

1 cup (250 mL): 325 Calories; 10.7 g Total Fat (2.9 g Mono, 2.8 g Poly, 2.4 g Sat); 11 mg Cholesterol; 52 g Carbohydrate; 7 g Fibre; 9 g Protein; 51 mg Sodium

 tip To toast grains, put grains into a shallow frying pan. Heat on medium for about five minutes, stirring often, until golden. Remember not to toast more than one type of grain at a time, because some types may take longer to toast than others.

Salsa Corn Waffles

Ándale (let's go)! It's morning time and you need a little heat to get you on your feet! Mild salsa flavours and sweet corn in a waffle are sure to do the trick. Top with salsa and sour cream.

Cracked wheat	1/4 cup	60 mL
Salt	1/4 tsp.	1 mL
Boiling water	1 cup	250 mL
Whole-wheat flour	1 1/2 cups	375 mL
All-purpose flour	1/2 cup	125 mL
Granulated sugar	1 tbsp.	15 mL
Baking powder	2 tsp.	10 mL
Baking soda	1 tsp.	5 mL
Pepper	1/2 tsp.	2 mL
Large eggs	2	2
Milk	1 1/2 cups	375 mL
Salsa	1/3 cup	75 mL
Butter (or hard margarine), melted	1/4 cup	60 mL
Frozen kernel corn, thawed	1 cup	250 mL

Combine wheat and salt in small heatproof bowl. Add boiling water. Stir. Let stand, covered, for 5 minutes. Drain. Set aside.

Combine next 6 ingredients in large bowl. Make a well in centre.

Whisk next 4 ingredients in medium bowl. Add corn and wheat. Stir. Add to well. Stir until just moistened. Batter will be lumpy. Preheat waffle iron. Spray with cooking spray. Pour batter onto waffle iron, using 1/2 to 3/4 cup (125 to 175 mL) for each waffle. Cook for 3 to 4 minutes per batch until browned and crisp. Transfer to plate. Cover to keep warm. Repeat with remaining batter, spraying waffle iron with cooking spray if necessary to prevent sticking. Makes about 6 Belgian waffles or 10 regular waffles.

1 Belgian waffle: 321 Calories; 10.8 g Total Fat (3.0 g Mono, 0.9 g Poly, 5.9 g Sat); 85 mg Cholesterol; 47 g Carbohydrate; 6 g Fibre; 11 g Protein; 458 mg Sodium

Buckwheat Apricot Pancakes

Good morning, sunshine! Make sure your day is warm and bright right from the start
with these golden pancakes with sweet bits of apricot. Great with apricot jam or syrup.

All-purpose flour	1 1/4 cups	300 mL
Buckwheat flour	3/4 cup	175 mL
Granulated sugar	1/4 cup	60 mL
Baking soda	2 tsp.	10 mL
Ground cardamom	1/4 tsp.	1 mL
Salt	1/4 tsp.	1 mL
Large eggs, fork-beaten	3	3
Can of apricot halves in light syrup, drained and syrup reserved, chopped	14 oz.	398 mL
Milk	1 cup	250 mL
Reserved apricot syrup	1/4 cup	60 mL
Canola oil	2 tbsp.	30 mL

Combine first 6 ingredients in large bowl. Make a well in centre.

Combine remaining 5 ingredients in medium bowl. Add to well. Stir until
just moistened. Batter will be lumpy. Preheat griddle to medium-high (see
Note). Reduce heat to medium. Spray with cooking spray. Pour batter onto
griddle, using about 1/3 cup (75 mL) for each pancake. Cook for about
2 minutes until bubbles form on top and edges appear dry. Turn pancake
over. Cook for about 2 minutes until golden. Remove to plate. Cover to
keep warm. Repeat with remaining batter, spraying griddle with cooking
spray if necessary to prevent sticking. Makes about 12 pancakes.

1 pancake: 156 Calories; 4.1 g Total Fat (2.0 g Mono, 1.0 g Poly, 0.8 g Sat); 47 mg Cholesterol;
26 g Carbohydrate; 1 g Fibre; 5 g Protein; 288 mg Sodium

Note: If you don't have an electric griddle, use a large frying pan. Heat
1 tsp. (5 mL) canola oil on medium. Heat more canola oil with each batch
if necessary to prevent sticking.

 For recipes that call for a small amount of cooked grains, we
recommend making one of the amounts given in Cooking
Grains *au Naturel*, pages 9-12, and freezing the remainder for
use in other recipes.

Almond Buckwheat Granola

Making homemade granola is easy and delicious! Keep this hearty, sweet and nutty breakfast staple on hand to serve with milk or over yogurt.

Large flake rolled oats	2 cups	500 mL
Whole buckwheat	2 cups	500 mL
Sliced natural almonds	1 cup	250 mL
Raw sunflower seeds	1/4 cup	60 mL
Sesame seeds	1/4 cup	60 mL
Brown sugar, packed	1/4 cup	60 mL
Canola oil	1/4 cup	60 mL
Honey	1/4 cup	60 mL
Almond extract	1 tsp.	5 mL
Ground cinnamon	1 tsp.	5 mL

Combine first 5 ingredients in large bowl.

Combine remaining 5 ingredients in small saucepan. Heat and stir on medium for about 2 minutes until brown sugar is dissolved. Add to oat mixture. Stir until coated. Spread evenly on 2 ungreased baking sheets with sides. Bake on separate racks in 325°F (160°C) oven for about 20 minutes, stirring occasionally and switching positions of baking sheets at halftime, until golden. Let stand on baking sheet until cool. Makes about 6 cups (1.5 L).

1 cup (250 mL): 572 Calories; 25.2 g Total Fat (12.5 g Mono, 7.2 g Poly, 2.8 g Sat); 0 mg Cholesterol; 75 g Carbohydrate; 8 g Fibre; 15 g Protein; 12 mg Sodium

Variation: Add 2 cups (500 mL) puffed wheat cereal to granola after baking.

1. Buckwheat Shrimp Crostini, page 24
2. Cracked Wheat Dolmades, page 20
3. Couscous-Stuffed Peppers, page 22
4. Salmon Quinoa Lettuce Cups, page 28

Props courtesy of: Pier 1 Imports

Buckwheat Sunrise

Watch out, oatmeal! Tangy orange and cranberry turn buckwheat into a serious contender for favourite breakfast grain. Make this the night before for a fast breakfast in the morning.

Water	1 1/2 cups	375 mL
Whole buckwheat	1 cup	250 mL
Grated orange zest	1 tsp.	5 mL
Salt	1/4 tsp.	1 mL
Orange juice	1 cup	250 mL
Chopped dried apricot	1/3 cup	75 mL
Dried cranberries	1/3 cup	75 mL
Liquid honey	3 tbsp.	50 mL
Slivered almonds, toasted (see Tip, page 28)	1/4 cup	60 mL

Combine first 4 ingredients in medium saucepan. Bring to a boil. Reduce heat to medium-low. Simmer, covered, for about 15 minutes, without stirring, until buckwheat is tender.

Add orange juice. Stir. Add next 3 ingredients. Stir. Transfer to medium bowl. Cool at room temperature before covering. Chill for at least 6 hours or overnight until apricot and cranberries are softened and liquid is absorbed.

Add almonds. Stir. Makes about 3 cups (750 mL).

1 cup (250 mL): 367 Calories; 6.1 g Total Fat (3.3 g Mono, 1.6 g Poly, 0.7 g Sat); 0 mg Cholesterol; 76 g Carbohydrate; 6 g Fibre; 8 g Protein; 210 mg Sodium

Pictured at left.

Variation: Instead of dried cranberries, use same amount of chopped dried cherries.

1. Millet Sweet Potato Cakes, page 39
2. Buckwheat Sunrise, above
3. Multi-Grain Pancakes, page 38

Props courtesy of: Stokes
Danesco Inc.
Canadian Tire

Multi-Grain Pancakes

These vanilla and cinnamon-flavoured pancakes pack enough whole-grain goodness to keep you going all morning long.

Whole-wheat flour	3/4 cup	175 mL
All-purpose flour	1/2 cup	125 mL
Brown sugar, packed	1/4 cup	60 mL
Large flake rolled oats	1/4 cup	60 mL
Yellow cornmeal	1/4 cup	60 mL
Baking powder	2 tsp.	10 mL
Ground cinnamon	1 tsp.	5 mL
Ground ginger	1 tsp.	5 mL
Baking soda	1/2 tsp.	2 mL
Salt	1/4 tsp.	1 mL
Large egg, fork-beaten	1	1
Buttermilk (or soured milk, see Tip, below)	1 1/2 cups	375 mL
Canola oil	2 tbsp.	30 mL
Vanilla extract	1 tsp.	5 mL

Combine first 10 ingredients in large bowl. Make a well in centre.

Combine remaining 4 ingredients in medium bowl. Add to well. Stir until just moistened. Batter will be lumpy. Preheat griddle to medium-high (see Note). Reduce heat to medium. Spray with cooking spray. Pour batter onto griddle, using about 1/3 cup (75 mL) for each pancake. Cook for about 2 minutes until bubbles form on top and edges appear dry. Turn pancake over. Cook for about 2 minutes until browned. Remove to plate. Cover to keep warm. Repeat with remaining batter, spraying griddle with cooking spray if necessary to prevent sticking. Makes about 10 pancakes.

1 pancake: 145 Calories; 4.0 g Total Fat (2.0 g Mono, 1.1 g Poly, 0.6 g Sat); 20 mg Cholesterol; 23 g Carbohydrate; 2 g Fibre; 4 g Protein; 222 mg Sodium

Pictured on page 36.

Note: If you don't have an electric griddle, use a large frying pan. Heat 1 tsp. (5 mL) canola oil on medium. Heat more canola oil with each batch if necessary to prevent sticking.

 tip To make soured milk, measure 1 tbsp. (15 mL) white vinegar or lemon juice into a 1 cup (250 mL) liquid measure. Add enough milk to make 1 cup (250 mL). Stir. Let stand for 1 minute.

Millet Sweet Potato Cakes

Think millet is for the birds? Smoky sausage, sweet potato and millet make these moist little cakes something to chirp about. (Parchment paper is required to keep these patties from sticking.)

Grated fresh peeled orange-fleshed sweet potato	2 cups	500 mL
Cooked millet (see page 11)	2 cups	500 mL
Finely chopped smoked ham sausage	1 cup	250 mL
Finely chopped celery	3/4 cup	175 mL
Finely chopped green onion	1/2 cup	125 mL
Large eggs	3	3
Whole-wheat flour	2 tbsp.	30 mL
Cajun seasoning	1 tbsp.	15 mL
Cooking spray		

Spread sweet potato on microwave-safe plate. Microwave, covered, on high (100%) for about 3 minutes until soft. Let stand until cool enough to handle. Squeeze sweet potato with paper towel to remove excess moisture. Place in large bowl.

Add next 4 ingredients. Mix well.

Whisk next 3 ingredients in small bowl. Add to sweet potato mixture. Stir well. Drop, using 1/3 cup (75 mL) for each cake, about 2 inches (2.5 cm) apart onto parchment paper-lined baking sheet with sides. Flatten into 3 inch (7.5 cm) diameter patties.

Spray patties with cooking spray. Bake in 400°F (205°C) oven for about 20 minutes until crisp and golden. Makes 12 cakes.

1 cake: 120 Calories; 4.1 g Total Fat (1.8 g Mono, 0.7 g Poly, 1.3 g Sat); 56 mg Cholesterol; 16 g Carbohydrate; 2 g Fibre; 5 g Protein; 247 mg Sodium

Pictured on page 36.

Knotty Cinnamon Buns

Sometimes it's nice to be a little bit knotty. Soothe the cravings of your sweet tooth with this whole-wheat cinnamon treat.

Butter (or hard margarine)	2 tbsp.	30 mL
Granulated sugar	1 1/2 tbsp.	25 mL
Salt	1 tsp.	5 mL
Hot water	1 cup	250 mL
Warm water	1/4 cup	60 mL
Granulated sugar	1 tbsp.	15 mL
Envelope of active dry yeast	1/4 oz.	8 g
(or 2 1/4 tsp., 11 mL)		
Whole-wheat flour	1 1/2 cups	375 mL
Large egg, fork-beaten	1	1
All-purpose flour	2 1/4 cups	550 mL
Granulated sugar	1/2 cup	125 mL
Ground cinnamon	3/4 tsp.	4 mL
Butter (or hard margarine), melted	3 tbsp.	50 mL

Measure first 3 ingredients into large bowl. Add hot water. Stir until butter is melted. Cool to room temperature.

Stir warm water and second amount of sugar in small bowl until sugar is dissolved. Sprinkle yeast over top. Let stand for 10 minutes. Stir until yeast is dissolved.

Add whole-wheat flour to butter mixture. Beat until smooth.

Add egg, all-purpose flour and yeast mixture. Mix until soft dough forms. Turn out onto lightly floured surface. Knead for 5 to 10 minutes until smooth and elastic. Place in greased extra-large bowl, turning once to grease top. Cover with greased waxed paper and tea towel. Let stand in oven with light on and door closed for about 1 hour until doubled in bulk. Punch dough down. Turn out onto lightly floured surface. Divide into 12 equal portions. Roll 1 portion into 10 inch (25 cm) long rope.

Combine third amount of sugar and cinnamon on plate.

(continued on next page)

Brush rope with melted butter. Press into sugar mixture until coated. Form into simple knot. Place in greased 9 x 13 inch (22 x 33 cm) pan. Repeat with remaining dough, butter and sugar mixture. Cover with greased waxed paper and tea towel. Let stand in oven with light on and door closed for about 30 minutes until doubled in size. Bake in 375°F (190°C) oven for about 30 minutes until golden brown. Makes 12 buns.

1 bun: 227 Calories; 5.7 g Total Fat (1.5 g Mono, 0.5 g Poly, 3.2 g Sat); 28 mg Cholesterol; 40 g Carbohydrate; 3 g Fibre; 5 g Protein; 235 mg Sodium

Pictured on page 54.

Quinoa Jam-Filled Muffins

Fancy yourself a treasure hunter? Well, you won't have to dig deep to unearth the golden apricot booty stowed in the centre of these not-too-sweet muffins.

All-purpose flour	1 cup	250 mL
Whole-wheat flour	1 cup	250 mL
Brown sugar, packed	3 tbsp.	50 mL
Baking powder	1 1/2 tsp.	7 mL
Salt	3/4 tsp.	4 mL
Baking soda	1/8 tsp.	0.5 mL
Large egg, fork-beaten	1	1
Cooked quinoa (see page 11)	1 1/2 cups	375 mL
Buttermilk (or soured milk, see Tip, page 38)	1 cup	250 mL
Raisins	1 cup	250 mL
Butter (or hard margarine), melted	1/4 cup	60 mL
Maple (or maple-flavoured) syrup	1/4 cup	60 mL
Apricot jam	1/4 cup	60 mL

Measure first 6 ingredients into large bowl. Stir. Make a well in centre.

Combine next 6 ingredients in small bowl. Add to well. Stir until just moistened. Fill 12 greased muffin cups 2/3 full. Make a small dent in batter with back of spoon.

Spoon 1 tsp. (5 mL) jam into each dent. Spoon remaining batter over top. Bake in 375°F (190°C) oven for about 25 minutes until firm to the touch. Let stand in pan for 5 minutes. Remove muffins from pan and place on wire rack to cool. Makes 12 muffins.

1 muffin: 239 Calories; 5.2 g Total Fat (1.3 g Mono, 0.4 g Poly, 2.7 g Sat); 26 mg Cholesterol; 45 g Carbohydrate; 3 g Fibre; 5 g Protein; 264 mg Sodium

Six-Grain Focaccia

You've got six reasons to love this tender bread with plenty of olive flavour.
We'll let you count the ways!

Warm water	1 1/4 cups	300 mL
Granulated sugar	1 tsp.	5 mL
Envelope of active dry yeast	1/4 oz.	8 g
(or 2 1/4 tsp., 11 mL)		
All-purpose flour	1 cup	250 mL
Whole-Grain Cereal Blend, page 15	1 cup	250 mL
Whole-wheat flour	1 cup	250 mL
Salt	1 tsp.	5 mL
Olive oil	2 tbsp.	30 mL
All-purpose flour, approximately	1/3 cup	75 mL
Olive oil	1 tsp.	5 mL
Olive oil	1 tsp.	5 mL
Coarsely chopped kalamata olives	1/2 cup	125 mL

Stir warm water and sugar in small bowl until sugar is dissolved. Sprinkle yeast over top. Let stand for 10 minutes. Stir until yeast is dissolved.

Combine next 4 ingredients in large bowl. Add first amount of olive oil and yeast mixture. Mix until soft dough forms. Turn out onto lightly floured surface. Knead for about 10 minutes until smooth and elastic, adding second amount of all-purpose flour 1 tbsp. (15 mL) at a time, if necessary, to prevent sticking. Place in greased extra-large bowl, turning once to grease top. Cover with greased waxed paper and tea towel. Let stand in oven with light on and door closed for about 35 minutes until doubled in bulk. Punch dough down. Turn out onto lightly floured surface. Knead for about 1 minute until smooth. Let stand for 10 minutes.

Coat 10 x 15 inch (25 x 38 cm) baking sheet with sides with second amount of olive oil. Gently press dough to fit dimensions of baking sheet. Cover with greased waxed paper and tea towel. Let stand in oven with light on and door closed for about 30 minutes until doubled in size.

Poke indentations on surface of dough with fingers. Brush with third amount of olive oil. Sprinkle olives over top. Bake in 400°F (205°C) oven for about 15 minutes until lightly browned. Remove bread from pan and place on wire rack to cool. Cuts into 12 squares.

(continued on next page)

Breads

1 square: 178 Calories; 4.5 g Total Fat (2.8 g Mono, 0.7 g Poly, 0.7 g Sat); 0 mg Cholesterol; 30 g Carbohydrate; 3 g Fibre; 5 g Protein; 246 mg Sodium

HERBED FOCACCIA BREAD: Combine 1 tsp. (5 mL) dried rosemary, crushed, 1/2 tsp. (2 mL) dried basil, 1/4 tsp. (1 mL) dried oregano and 1/8 tsp. (0.5 mL) dried thyme. Add to flour mixture.

Amaranth Banana Bread

Our second name choice was Amarananana Bread! Amaranth makes a superb addition to banana bread. Don't be tempted to cut the baking time short—this loaf needs a full hour in the oven.

All-purpose flour	2 cups	500 mL
Ground cinnamon	1 1/2 tsp.	7 mL
Baking powder	1 tsp.	5 mL
Baking soda	1 tsp.	5 mL
Salt	1/2 tsp.	2 mL
Butter (or hard margarine), softened	1/3 cup	75 mL
Granulated sugar	3/4 cup	175 mL
Cooked amaranth (see Tip, page 33)	1 cup	250 mL
Mashed overripe banana	1 cup	250 mL
Large eggs	2	2
Buttermilk (or soured milk, see Tip, page 38)	1/2 cup	125 mL

Measure first 5 ingredients into large bowl. Stir. Make a well in centre.

Cream butter and sugar in medium bowl.

Add amaranth and banana. Mix until no clumps of amaranth remain. Add eggs and buttermilk. Beat well. Add to well. Stir until just moistened. Spread in greased 9 x 5 x 3 inch (22 x 12.5 x 7.5 cm) loaf pan. Bake in 375°F (190°C) oven for 1 hour. Wooden pick inserted in centre may still show some moistness, but loaf should be cracked on top and firm to the touch. Let stand in pan for 10 minutes. Remove loaf from pan and place on wire rack to cool. Cuts into 16 slices.

1 slice: 195 Calories; 5.3 g Total Fat (1.4 g Mono, 0.7 g Poly, 2.8 g Sat); 33 mg Cholesterol; 33 g Carbohydrate; 3 g Fibre; 5 g Protein; 213 mg Sodium

Pictured on page 54.

Dark Fennel Bread

Tall, dark and handsome—just what you're looking for in a bread. Invite this good-lookin' loaf on a dinner date and you won't be disappointed—it's beautiful on the inside, too! (Makes two loaves.)

Warm water	1/4 cup	60 mL
Granulated sugar	1 tsp.	5 mL
Envelope of active dry yeast	1/4 oz.	8 g
(or 2 1/4 tsp., 11 mL)		
Whole-wheat flour	2 1/2 cups	625 mL
Brown rice flour	1/2 cup	125 mL
Natural wheat bran	1/2 cup	125 mL
Cocoa, sifted if lumpy	1/4 cup	60 mL
Brown sugar, packed	2 tbsp.	30 mL
Salt	2 tsp.	10 mL
Fennel seed	1 tsp.	5 mL
Onion flakes	1 tsp.	5 mL
Warm water	1 1/2 cups	375 mL
Canola oil	1/4 cup	60 mL
Fancy (mild) molasses	1/4 cup	60 mL
Instant coffee granules	1 tbsp.	15 mL
All-purpose flour	2 cups	500 mL
All-purpose flour, approximately	3 tbsp.	50 mL
Fennel seed	1 tsp.	5 mL

Stir first amount of warm water and granulated sugar in small bowl until sugar is dissolved. Sprinkle yeast over top. Let stand for 10 minutes. Stir until yeast is dissolved.

Measure next 8 ingredients into large bowl.

Combine next 4 ingredients in separate small bowl. Add to flour mixture. Add yeast mixture. Mix well. Let stand for 10 minutes.

(continued on next page)

Add first amount of all-purpose flour. Mix until soft dough forms. Turn out onto lightly floured surface. Knead for 5 to 10 minutes until smooth and elastic, adding second amount of all-purpose flour 1 tbsp. (15 mL) at a time, if necessary, to prevent sticking. Place in greased extra-large bowl, turning once to grease top. Cover with greased waxed paper and tea towel. Let stand in oven with light on and door closed for about 1 hour until doubled in bulk. Punch dough down. Turn out onto lightly floured surface. Knead for about 1 minute until smooth. Divide into 2 equal portions. Roll each portion into a ball.

Spread half of second amount of fennel seed on large plate. Press top of 1 ball into fennel seed. Place, seed-side up, on greased baking sheet. Repeat with remaining fennel seed and second ball. Place on same baking sheet. Cover with greased waxed paper and tea towel. Let stand in oven with light on and door closed for about 40 minutes until doubled in size. Bake in 350°F (175°C) oven for about 30 minutes until hollow sounding when tapped. Remove loaves from baking sheet and place on wire racks to cool. Each loaf cuts into 12 slices, for a total of 24 slices.

1 slice: *136 Calories; 2.9 g Total Fat (1.5 g Mono, 0.9 g Poly, 0.3 g Sat); 0 mg Cholesterol; 26 g Carbohydrate; 3 g Fibre; 4 g Protein; 198 mg Sodium*

Pictured on page 53.

Paré Pointer

When moths want to see a floor show, they eat a hole in the rug.

Chai, Millet and Rice Biscuits

Need a boost? Chai tea spices give these tender drop biscuits a boost that is sure to raise your spirits. Serve with savoury soups or sweet condiments like jam or honey.

All-purpose flour	2 cups	500 mL
Granulated sugar	3 tbsp.	50 mL
Baking powder	2 tsp.	10 mL
Ground ginger	1 tsp.	5 mL
Baking soda	1/2 tsp.	2 mL
Ground cardamom	1/4 tsp.	1 mL
Ground cinnamon	1/4 tsp.	1 mL
Salt	1/2 tsp.	2 mL
Pepper	1/4 tsp.	1 mL
Ground cloves	1/8 tsp.	0.5 mL
Ground nutmeg	1/8 tsp.	0.5 mL
Cold butter (or hard margarine), cut up	1/2 cup	125 mL
Large egg, fork-beaten	1	1
Cold cooked millet (see page 11)	1 cup	250 mL
Cold cooked wild rice (see Tip, page 33)	1 cup	250 mL
Buttermilk (or soured milk, see Tip, page 38)	2/3 cup	150 mL

Combine first 11 ingredients in large bowl. Cut in butter until mixture resembles coarse crumbs. Make a well in centre.

Add remaining 4 ingredients to well. Stir until just moistened. Drop, using 1/4 cup (60 mL) for each biscuit, about 2 inches (5 cm) apart onto greased baking sheet. Bake in 400°F (205°C) oven for about 15 minutes until golden and wooden pick inserted in centre comes out clean. Let stand on baking sheet for 5 minutes. Remove biscuits from baking sheet and place on wire rack to cool. Makes 15 biscuits.

1 biscuit: 162 Calories; 7.2 g Total Fat (1.9 g Mono, 0.5 g Poly, 4.3 g Sat); 30 mg Cholesterol; 21 g Carbohydrate; 1 g Fibre; 3 g Protein; 216 mg Sodium

Pictured on page 72 and on back cover.

Cornmeal Pepper Lime Scones

These golden-yellow scones have a flavour that's absolutely superb! Waste naught, want naught—use the juice from your lime to make soured milk for this recipe.

All-purpose flour	1 cup	250 mL
Whole-wheat flour	1 cup	250 mL
Grated Monterey Jack cheese	1/2 cup	125 mL
Yellow cornmeal	1/2 cup	125 mL
Granulated sugar	2 tbsp.	30 mL
Baking powder	2 tsp.	10 mL
Grated lime zest	2 tsp.	10 mL
Baking soda	1/2 tsp.	2 mL
Salt	1/2 tsp.	2 mL
Pepper	1 tsp.	5 mL
Cold butter (or hard margarine), cut up	1/2 cup	125 mL
Large egg, fork-beaten	1	1
Buttermilk (or soured milk, see Tip, page 38)	1 cup	250 mL

Combine first 10 ingredients in large bowl. Cut in butter until mixture resembles coarse crumbs. Make a well in centre.

Add egg and buttermilk to well. Stir until just moistened. Drop, using 1/3 cup (75 mL) for each scone, about 2 inches (5 cm) apart onto greased baking sheet. Bake in 400°F (205°C) oven for about 20 minutes until golden and wooden pick inserted in centre comes out clean. Let stand on baking sheet for 5 minutes. Remove scones from baking sheet and place on wire rack to cool. Makes 12 scones.

1 scone: 201 Calories; 10.0 g Total Fat (2.7 g Mono, 0.6 g Poly, 6.0 g Sat); 40 mg Cholesterol; 23 g Carbohydrate; 2 g Fibre; 5 g Protein; 300 mg Sodium

Pictured on page 108.

Granola Soda Bread

Granola, that homey staple, steps out and adds an air of intrigue to your soda bread. A dusting of sugar adds a sweet and glittery touch. You will need Almond Buckwheat Granola, page 34, for this recipe.

All-purpose flour	3 cups	750 mL
Whole-wheat flour	1 cup	250 mL
Granulated sugar	1/4 cup	60 mL
Baking powder	1 tbsp.	15 mL
Baking soda	1 tsp.	5 mL
Salt	1 tsp.	5 mL
Cold butter (or hard margarine), cut up	1/4 cup	60 mL
Almond Buckwheat Granola, page 34	1 cup	250 mL
Large egg	1	1
Buttermilk (or soured milk, see Tip, page 38)	2 cups	500 mL
Almond extract	1/4 tsp.	1 mL
Melted butter	1 tbsp.	15 mL
Granulated sugar	1 tbsp.	15 mL

Combine first 6 ingredients in large bowl. Cut in butter until mixture resembles coarse crumbs.

Add Almond Buckwheat Granola. Stir. Make a well in centre.

Whisk next 3 ingredients in small bowl. Add to well. Stir until soft dough forms. Transfer to greased 9 inch (22 cm) round pan. Press or pat out to edge of pan. Cut '+' on top of dough, making cuts about 5 inches (12.5 cm) long and 1/2 inch (12 mm) deep, using sharp knife.

Brush with melted butter. Sprinkle with second amount of sugar. Bake in 350°F (175°C) oven for about 45 minutes until golden and wooden pick inserted in centre comes out clean. Let stand in pan for 5 minutes. Remove bread from pan and place on wire rack to cool. Cuts into 8 wedges.

1 wedge: 421 Calories; 12.1 g Total Fat (3.9 g Mono, 1.6 g Poly, 5.5 g Sat); 44 mg Cholesterol; 67 g Carbohydrate; 4 g Fibre; 12 g Protein; 673 mg Sodium

Cheddar Onion Muffins

Zippy jalapeño jelly adds its fiery sweetness to savoury Cheddar and green onions in these moist muffins. A super side for soup, salad or chili.

Brown rice flour	1 cup	250 mL
Yellow cornmeal	1/2 cup	125 mL
Ground flaxseed (see Tip, below)	2 tbsp.	30 mL
Baking powder	1 tsp.	5 mL
Baking soda	1/2 tsp.	2 mL
Salt	1/4 tsp.	1 mL
Large eggs, fork-beaten	2	2
Light sour cream	1/2 cup	125 mL
Milk	1/4 cup	60 mL
Canola oil	3 tbsp.	50 mL
Granulated sugar	2 tbsp.	30 mL
Red (or green) jalapeño jelly	2 tbsp.	30 mL
Chopped green onion	1/2 cup	125 mL
Grated sharp Cheddar cheese	1/2 cup	125 mL
Red (or green) jalapeño jelly, melted	1 tbsp.	15 mL

Measure first 6 ingredients into large bowl. Stir. Make a well in centre.

Combine next 6 ingredients in medium bowl. Add to well.

Add green onion and cheese. Stir until just moistened. Fill 12 greased muffin cups half full. Bake in 375°F (190°C) oven for about 15 minutes until wooden pick inserted in centre of muffin comes out clean.

Brush second amount of jelly over muffins. Let stand in pan for 5 minutes. Remove muffins from pan and place on wire rack to cool. Makes 12 muffins.

1 muffin: 170 Calories; 7.6 g Total Fat (3.0 g Mono, 1.4 g Poly, 2.1 g Sat); 39 mg Cholesterol; 20 g Carbohydrate; 1 g Fibre; 5 g Protein; 175 mg Sodium

 tip Grind 2 1/2 tbsp. (37 mL) whole flaxseed in blender or coffee grinder to yield 1/4 cup (60 mL) ground flaxseed. Store leftover ground flaxseed in airtight container in the refrigerator.

Peppery Dinner Pull-Aparts

Your dinner go-withs making your meal look a little lacklustre? Pep it up with these savoury, light-textured pull-aparts packed with artichoke and Parmesan. Best served warm.

Water	1 1/4 cups	300 mL
Cracked wheat	1/3 cup	75 mL
Reserved liquid from artichoke hearts	1/4 cup	60 mL
Granulated sugar	4 tsp.	20 mL
Salt	1 tsp.	5 mL
Whole-wheat flour	2 cups	500 mL
Envelope of instant yeast	1/4 oz.	8 g
(or 2 1/4 tsp., 11 mL)		
Large egg, fork-beaten	1	1
Jar of marinated artichoke hearts, drained and liquid reserved, chopped	12 oz.	340 mL
All-purpose flour	1 3/4 cups	425 mL
All-purpose flour, approximately	1/2 cup	125 mL
Butter	1 tbsp.	15 mL
Olive oil	1 tbsp.	15 mL
Grated Parmesan cheese	1/2 cup	125 mL
Coarsely ground pepper	1 tsp.	5 mL

Combine first 5 ingredients in small saucepan. Bring to a boil. Remove from heat. Stir. Pour into large bowl. Let stand, uncovered, for 25 minutes.

Combine whole-wheat flour and yeast in small bowl. Add to wheat mixture. Beat until well mixed.

Add egg and artichoke. Stir well.

Add first amount of all-purpose flour, 1/2 cup (125 mL) at a time, stirring well after each addition until stiff dough forms. Turn out onto lightly floured surface. Knead for 5 to 10 minutes until smooth and elastic, adding second amount of all-purpose flour 1 tbsp. (15 mL) at a time, if necessary, to prevent sticking. Place in greased large bowl, turning once to grease top. Cover with greased waxed paper and tea towel. Let stand in oven with light on and door closed for 30 minutes.

(continued on next page)

50

Heat butter and olive oil in small saucepan on low heat until butter is melted. Cool slightly.

Combine cheese and pepper in small bowl. Turn out dough onto lightly floured surface. Divide into 18 equal portions. Arrange 6 portions in single layer in greased 12 cup (3 L) bundt pan. Drizzle with 1/3 butter mixture. Sprinkle with 1/3 cheese mixture. Arrange another 6 dough portions on top to make second layer. Drizzle with 1/3 butter mixture. Sprinkle with 1/3 cheese mixture. Repeat with remaining dough portions, butter mixture, and cheese mixture. Cover with greased waxed paper and tea towel. Let stand in oven with light on and door closed for about 1 hour until doubled in size. Bake in 350°F (175°C) oven for 40 to 45 minutes until golden. Loosen bread from pan and invert onto wire rack to cool. Makes 18 pieces.

1 piece: 164 Calories; 4.0 g Total Fat (1.1 g Mono, 0.3 g Poly, 1.2 g Sat); 14 mg Cholesterol; 27 g Carbohydrate; 3 g Fibre; 6 g Protein; 262 mg Sodium

Pictured on page 53.

Paré Pointer
A teacher says to spit out your gum while a train says to choo choo.

Savoury Drop Biscuits

Get ready to drop everything for these cheesy ham and onion biscuits. For those who prefer a less rustic, more refined look, these beauties can also be baked in muffin tins.

Rye flour	1 cup	250 mL
All-purpose flour	1/2 cup	125 mL
Whole-wheat flour	1/2 cup	125 mL
Baking powder	1 tbsp.	15 mL
Granulated sugar	1 tbsp.	15 mL
Caraway seed	1/2 tsp.	2 mL
Salt	1/2 tsp.	2 mL
Pepper	1/4 tsp.	1 mL
Large egg, fork-beaten	1	1
Milk	1 cup	250 mL
Grated Swiss cheese	1/2 cup	125 mL
Finely chopped onion	1/3 cup	75 mL
Finely diced Black Forest ham	1/4 cup	60 mL
Canola oil	2 tbsp.	30 mL

Measure first 8 ingredients into large bowl. Stir. Make a well in centre.

Combine remaining 6 ingredients in medium bowl. Add to well. Stir until just moistened. Drop, using 1/4 cup (60 mL) for each biscuit, about 2 inches (5 cm) apart onto greased baking sheet. Bake in 400°F (205°C) oven for 18 to 20 minutes until wooden pick inserted in centre comes out clean. Let stand on baking sheet for 5 minutes. Remove biscuits from baking sheet and place on wire rack to cool. Makes 12 biscuits.

1 biscuit: 130 Calories; 4.7 g Total Fat (2.1 g Mono, 1.0 g Poly, 1.4 g Sat); 22 mg Cholesterol; 17 g Carbohydrate; 2 g Fibre; 5 g Protein; 231 mg Sodium

Pictured on page 72 and on back cover.

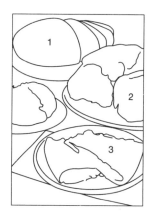

1. Dark Fennel Bread, page 44
2. Peppery Dinner Pull-Aparts, page 50
3. Wheat Calzone, page 116

Props courtesy of: Winners Stores
Cherison Enterprises Inc.
The Bay

Orange Poppy Seed Muffins

Cornmeal muffins are great, but add a little zesty orange and they'll put a real pop in your hop.

All-purpose flour	1 cup	250 mL
Whole-wheat flour	3/4 cup	175 mL
Yellow cornmeal	3/4 cup	175 mL
Poppy seeds	3 tbsp.	50 mL
Baking powder	1 tbsp.	15 mL
Baking soda	1/2 tsp.	2 mL
Salt	1/2 tsp.	2 mL
Large eggs, fork-beaten	2	2
Grated zucchini (with peel)	1 cup	250 mL
Liquid honey	1/2 cup	125 mL
Orange juice	1/2 cup	125 mL
Canola oil	1/3 cup	75 mL
Grated orange zest	1 tsp.	5 mL

Measure first 7 ingredients into large bowl. Stir. Make a well in centre.

Combine remaining 6 ingredients in medium bowl. Add to well. Stir until just moistened. Fill 12 greased muffin cups 3/4 full. Bake in 375°F (190°C) oven for 18 to 20 minutes until wooden pick inserted in centre of muffin comes out clean. Let stand in pan for 5 minutes. Remove muffins from pan and place on wire rack to cool. Makes 12 muffins.

1 muffin: 206 Calories; 8.0 g Total Fat (4.0 g Mono, 2.7 g Poly, 0.8 g Sat); 31 mg Cholesterol; 30 g Carbohydrate; 2 g Fibre; 4 g Protein; 228 mg Sodium

Pictured at left.

1. Orange Poppy Seed Muffins, above
2. Knotty Cinnamon Buns, page 40
3. Amaranth Banana Bread, page 43

Multi-Grain Muffins

These lightly pumpkin-flavoured, multi-grain muffins are best munched in multiples!

All-purpose flour	1 1/2 cups	375 mL
Large flake rolled oats	3/4 cup	175 mL
Whole-wheat flour	3/4 cup	175 mL
Quinoa (see Note), toasted (see Tip, page 31)	1/2 cup	125 mL
Baking powder	2 1/2 tsp.	12 mL
Baking soda	1 tsp.	5 mL
Ground cinnamon	1 tsp.	5 mL
Salt	1/2 tsp.	2 mL
Large eggs, fork-beaten	2	2
Can of pure pumpkin (no spices)	14 oz.	398 mL
Buttermilk (or soured milk, see Tip, page 38)	1 cup	250 mL
Brown sugar, packed	1/2 cup	125 mL
Canola oil	1/2 cup	125 mL
Liquid honey	1/4 cup	60 mL
Vanilla extract	1 tsp.	5 mL
TOPPING		
Unsalted, roasted shelled pumpkin seeds	3 tbsp.	50 mL
Unsalted, roasted sunflower seeds	3 tbsp.	50 mL

Measure first 8 ingredients into large bowl. Stir. Make a well in centre.

Combine next 7 ingredients in medium bowl. Add to well. Stir until just moistened. Fill 18 greased muffin cups 3/4 full.

Topping: Combine pumpkin seeds and sunflower seeds in small cup. Sprinkle over batter. Bake in 375°F (190°C) oven for 18 to 20 minutes until wooden pick inserted in centre of muffin comes out clean. Let stand in pan for 5 minutes. Remove muffins from pan and place on wire rack to cool. Makes 18 muffins.

1 muffin: 222 Calories; 9.2 g Total Fat (4.5 g Mono, 3.1 g Poly, 1.1 g Sat); 21 mg Cholesterol; 31 g Carbohydrate; 3 g Fibre; 5 g Protein; 198 mg Sodium

Note: Do not rinse quinoa before toasting.

Tabbouleh

Tabbouleh (pronounced tah-BOO-luh) is a traditional Lebanese salad whose green comes from parsley and green onions. Great as a side with grilled meats or served with crisp bread.

Bulgur, fine grind	1/3 cup	75 mL
Water, to cover		
Finely chopped fresh parsley	2 cups	500 mL
Finely chopped English cucumber (with peel)	1 cup	250 mL
Finely chopped tomato	3/4 cup	175 mL
Finely chopped red pepper	1/2 cup	125 mL
Finely chopped green onion	1/4 cup	60 mL
Finely chopped radish	1/4 cup	60 mL
Dried mint leaves	1 tsp.	5 mL
DRESSING		
Lemon juice	1/4 cup	60 mL
Olive oil	1 tbsp.	15 mL
Salt	1/2 tsp.	2 mL

Measure bulgur into small bowl. Add water. Stir. Let stand for about 20 minutes until tender. Drain well. Set aside.

Put next 7 ingredients into medium bowl. Toss.

Dressing: Combine remaining 3 ingredients in small cup. Drizzle over parsley mixture. Add bulgur. Toss until coated. Makes about 4 1/2 cups (1.1 L).

1 cup (250 mL): 88 Calories; 3.5 g Total Fat (2.3 g Mono, 0.4 g Poly, 0.5 g Sat); 0 mg Cholesterol; 14 g Carbohydrate; 2 g Fibre; 3 g Protein; 283 mg Sodium

Pictured on page 71.

Quinoa Salad

Make a dinner date with this unique salad that's chock full of crunchy almonds,
sweet dates and salty feta in a light lemon and honey dressing.

Water	2 1/4 cups	550 mL
Salt	1/8 tsp.	0.5 mL
Quinoa, rinsed and drained	1 1/2 cups	375 mL
Olive (or canola) oil	2 tsp.	10 mL
Finely chopped celery	1/2 cup	125 mL
Finely chopped onion	1/2 cup	125 mL
Chopped pitted dates	3/4 cup	175 mL
Crumbled light feta cheese	1/2 cup	125 mL
Slivered almonds, toasted (see Tip, page 28)	1/2 cup	125 mL
Chopped fresh chives	2 tbsp.	30 mL
Finely chopped fresh parsley (or 1 1/2 tsp., 7 mL, flakes)	2 tbsp.	30 mL

HONEY LEMON DRESSING

Lemon juice	3 tbsp.	50 mL
Liquid honey	2 tbsp.	30 mL
Olive (or canola) oil	1 tbsp.	15 mL
Salt	1/4 tsp.	1 mL
Pepper	1/8 tsp.	0.5 mL

Combine water and salt in large saucepan. Bring to a boil. Add quinoa. Stir. Reduce heat to medium-low. Simmer, covered, for about 20 minutes, without stirring, until quinoa is tender and liquid is absorbed. Transfer to large bowl.

Heat olive oil in small frying pan on medium. Add celery and onion. Cook for 5 to 10 minutes, stirring often, until onion is softened. Add to quinoa. Stir. Cool.

Add next 5 ingredients. Toss.

Honey Lemon Dressing: Combine all 5 ingredients in small cup. Makes about 1/3 cup (75 mL) dressing. Drizzle over quinoa mixture. Toss until coated. Makes about 6 cups (1.5 L).

1 cup (250 mL): 354 Calories; 11.6 g Total Fat (5.9 g Mono, 2.3 g Poly, 2.0 g Sat); 4 mg Cholesterol; 55 g Carbohydrate; 6 g Fibre; 11 g Protein; 318 mg Sodium

Pictured on page 71.

Spinach Rice Salad

Shall I compare thee to a summer's day? Thou art so fresh and delicious, it's true.
With a spiced apple dressing that's divine. Could a true salad lover ask for more?

APPLE SPICE DRESSING

Apple cider vinegar	1/4 cup	60 mL
Canola oil	1/4 cup	60 mL
Frozen concentrated apple juice, thawed	1/4 cup	60 mL
Garlic clove, minced	1	1
(or 1/4 tsp., 1 mL, powder)		
Ground cinnamon	1/4 tsp.	1 mL
Ground nutmeg	1/4 tsp.	1 mL
Salt	1/4 tsp.	1 mL
Pepper	1/4 tsp.	1 mL

SALAD

Cooked Wild and White Rice Blend, page 13	2 cups	500 mL
Sliced fresh white mushrooms	2 cups	500 mL
Cooked hard red wheat (see page 10)	1 cup	250 mL
Diced unpeeled cooking apple (such as McIntosh)	1 cup	250 mL
Chopped pecans, toasted (see Tip, page 28)	1/2 cup	125 mL
Diced yellow pepper	1/2 cup	125 mL
Fresh spinach leaves, lightly packed	3 cups	750 mL

Apple Spice Dressing: Combine all 8 ingredients in jar with tight-fitting lid. Shake well. Makes about 3/4 cup (175 mL) dressing.

Salad: Combine first 6 ingredients in large bowl. Drizzle dressing over top. Toss.

Add spinach. Toss. Makes about 9 1/2 cups (2.4 L).

1 cup (250 mL): 241 Calories; 10.9 g Total Fat (6.0 g Mono, 3.3 g Poly, 0.9 g Sat); 0 mg Cholesterol; 33 g Carbohydrate; 4 g Fibre; 6 g Protein; 117 mg Sodium

Pictured on front cover.

Nutty Wild Rice Salad

This fresh and nutty salad, which acts both as a starch and a vegetable, is guaranteed to win friends. Perfect at a barbecue.

Cooked wild rice (see page 12)	3 cups	750 mL
Halved cherry tomatoes	1 cup	250 mL
Chopped fresh parsley	1/2 cup	125 mL
Diced yellow pepper	1/2 cup	125 mL
Chopped green onion	1/3 cup	75 mL
Dried cranberries	1/3 cup	75 mL
Coarsely chopped pecans	1/4 cup	60 mL
RASPBERRY DRESSING		
Olive (or canola) oil	1/3 cup	75 mL
Raspberry vinegar	3 tbsp.	50 mL
Raspberry jam	2 tbsp.	30 mL
Dijon mustard	1 tsp.	5 mL
Garlic clove, minced	1	1
(or 1/4 tsp., 1 mL, powder)		
Salt	1/4 tsp.	1 mL
Pepper	1/4 tsp.	1 mL

Combine first 7 ingredients in large bowl.

Raspberry Dressing: Combine all 7 ingredients in small cup. Makes about 2/3 cup (150 mL) dressing. Drizzle over rice mixture. Toss. Makes about 6 cups (1.5 L).

1 cup (250 mL): 266 Calories; 15.4 g Total Fat (10.5 g Mono, 2.3 g Poly, 1.9 g Sat); 0 mg Cholesterol; 30 g Carbohydrate; 3 g Fibre; 4 g Protein; 116 mg Sodium

Pictured on page 71.

Wheat Walnut Salad

With walnuts, cranberries, blue cheese and a fresh rosemary dressing,
this salad is the epitome of bistro chic.

DRESSING

Olive (or canola) oil	3 tbsp.	50 mL
Red wine vinegar	3 tbsp.	50 mL
Finely chopped fresh rosemary	2 tsp.	10 mL
Salt	1/2 tsp.	2 mL
Pepper	1/4 tsp.	1 mL

SALAD

Cooked hard red wheat (see Tip, page 33)	2 cups	500 mL
Chopped walnuts, toasted (see Tip, page 28)	1/2 cup	125 mL
Dried cranberries	1/2 cup	125 mL
Crumbled blue cheese (about 1 1/2 oz., 43 g)	1/4 cup	60 mL

Dressing: Combine all 5 ingredients in jar with tight-fitting lid. Shake well.

Salad: Put wheat into medium bowl. Drizzle with dressing. Toss.

Add remaining 3 ingredients. Toss gently. Makes about 4 cups (1 L).

1 cup (250 mL): 588 Calories; 25.0 g Total Fat (10.0 g Mono, 8.9 g Poly, 4.6 g Sat); 8 mg Cholesterol; 80 g Carbohydrate; 14 g Fibre; 19 g Protein; 444 mg Sodium

Spicy Coconut Rice Soup

If you favour the flavour of coconut rice, then this coconut soup must be made for you.
Chock full of vegetables and shrimp, it comes with a spicy kick.

Canola oil	1 tsp.	5 mL
Chopped onion	1 cup	250 mL
Red curry paste	1 tsp.	5 mL
Prepared chicken broth	5 cups	1.25 L
Granulated sugar	1 tbsp.	15 mL
Soy sauce	1 tbsp.	15 mL
Wild rice	1/4 cup	60 mL
Long-grain brown rice	1/4 cup	60 mL
Can of cut baby corn, drained	14 oz.	398 mL
Sliced red pepper	1 cup	250 mL
Snow peas, trimmed and halved	1 cup	250 mL
Can of light coconut milk	14 oz.	398 mL
Medium shrimp (peeled and deveined)	1/2 lb.	225 g
Lime juice	1 tbsp.	15 mL

Heat canola oil in large saucepan on medium. Add onion. Cook, uncovered, for about 5 minutes, stirring often, until onion starts to soften.

Add curry paste. Heat and stir for about 1 minute until fragrant.

Add next 3 ingredients. Stir. Bring to a boil.

Add wild rice. Reduce heat to medium-low. Simmer, covered, for 30 minutes. Bring to a boil.

Add brown rice. Stir. Reduce heat to medium-low. Simmer, covered, for about 30 minutes until rice is tender.

Add next 3 ingredients. Stir. Simmer, covered, for about 3 minutes until vegetables are tender-crisp.

Add coconut milk and shrimp. Stir. Simmer, covered, for about 2 minutes until shrimp turn pink.

Add lime juice. Stir. Makes about 8 cups (2 L).

(continued on next page)

1 cup (250 mL): 216 Calories; 6.3 g Total Fat (1.0 g Mono, 1.0 g Poly, 3.3 g Sat); 43 mg Cholesterol; 29 g Carbohydrate; 3 g Fibre; 13 g Protein; 735 mg Sodium

Pictured on page 72 and on back cover.

Black Bean and Barley Soup

This hearty, southwestern-inspired soup is bound to bring out your inner cowboy or cowgirl. Yee-haw!

Canola oil	1 tbsp.	15 mL
Chopped onion	2 cups	500 mL
Chopped celery	1 1/2 cups	375 mL
Chopped red pepper	1 cup	250 mL
Garlic cloves, minced	2	2
(or 1/2 tsp., 2 mL, powder)		
Ground coriander	1/2 tsp.	2 mL
Ground cumin	1/2 tsp.	2 mL
Prepared chicken broth	8 cups	2 L
Can of black beans, rinsed and drained	19 oz.	540 mL
Pot barley	1/3 cup	75 mL
Bay leaves	2	2
Chopped fresh cilantro or parsley	2 tbsp.	30 mL

Heat canola oil in large saucepan or Dutch oven on medium. Add next 3 ingredients. Cook, uncovered, for about 10 minutes, stirring often, until onion is softened.

Add next 3 ingredients. Heat and stir for about 1 minute until fragrant.

Add broth and beans. Stir. Carefully process with hand blender or in blender until vegetables are finely chopped. Bring to a boil.

Add barley and bay leaves. Stir. Reduce heat to medium-low. Simmer, covered, for about 1 hour, stirring occasionally, until barley is tender. Discard bay leaves.

Add cilantro. Stir. Makes about 9 3/4 cups (2.4 L).

1 cup (250 mL): 160 Calories; 3.1 g Total Fat (1.3 g Mono, 0.8 g Poly, 0.5 g Sat); 0 mg Cholesterol; 23 g Carbohydrate; 6 g Fibre; 10 g Protein; 785 mg Sodium

Chicken Millet Chowder

Why did the potato cross the road? To make way for the millet in this creamy vegetable and chicken chowder.

Canola oil	2 tsp.	10 mL
Chopped celery	1 cup	250 mL
Chopped onion	1 cup	250 mL
Diced carrot	1 cup	250 mL
Chopped red pepper	1/2 cup	125 mL
Bay leaves	2	2
Celery salt	1/2 tsp.	2 mL
Pepper	1/4 tsp.	1 mL
Prepared chicken broth	4 cups	1 L
Millet	1/2 cup	125 mL
Milk	2 cups	500 mL
All-purpose flour	3 tbsp.	50 mL
Chopped cooked chicken	1 cup	250 mL
Frozen kernel corn	1 cup	250 mL
Fresh (or frozen) whole green beans, cut into 1 inch (2.5 cm) pieces	1/2 cup	125 mL

Heat canola oil in large saucepan or Dutch oven on medium. Add next 3 ingredients. Cook, uncovered, for about 5 minutes, stirring often, until onion starts to soften.

Add next 4 ingredients. Stir. Cook for about 2 minutes, stirring occasionally (see Note), until red pepper starts to soften.

Add broth. Bring to a boil. Add millet. Stir. Reduce heat to medium-low. Simmer, covered, for 30 minutes.

Whisk milk into flour in small bowl until smooth. Slowly add to broth mixture, stirring constantly, until boiling. Reduce heat to medium-low. Simmer, covered, for 10 minutes.

Add remaining 3 ingredients. Stir. Simmer, covered, for about 5 minutes until vegetables are tender. Discard bay leaves. Makes about 8 cups (2 L).

1 cup (250 mL): 249 Calories; 4.5 g Total Fat (1.6 g Mono, 1.3 g Poly, 1.1 g Sat); 17 mg Cholesterol; 38 g Carbohydrate; 3 g Fibre; 15 g Protein; 530 mg Sodium

Pictured on page 108.

Note: While stirring, be careful not to break up the bay leaves.

Avocado Rice Soup

The intriguing texture of creamy avocado and puréed wild rice is sure to add some cool to the hottest summer day. Garnish with a spoonful of salsa to add an extra dose of colour and flavour.

Chopped avocado	1 1/2 cups	375 mL
Lemon juice	2 tbsp.	30 mL
Prepared vegetable broth	3 cups	750 mL
Ground cumin	1/4 tsp.	1 mL
Wild rice	1/3 cup	75 mL
Chopped peeled English cucumber, seeds removed	1 cup	250 mL
Milk	1/2 cup	125 mL
Lemon juice	1 tbsp.	15 mL
Salt	1/2 tsp.	2 mL
Pepper	1/4 tsp.	1 mL

Combine avocado and lemon juice in medium bowl. Set aside.

Combine broth and cumin in medium saucepan. Bring to a boil. Add wild rice. Stir. Reduce heat to medium-low. Simmer, covered, for about 75 minutes until wild rice is tender. Remove from heat.

Add remaining 5 ingredients and avocado mixture. Carefully process with hand blender or in blender until smooth (see Safety Tip). Pour into large bowl. Cool to room temperature. Chill, covered, for about 3 hours until cold. Makes about 5 cups (1.25 L).

1 cup (250 mL): 134 Calories; 7.1 g Total Fat (4.5 g Mono, 0.9 g Poly, 1.1 g Sat); 1 mg Cholesterol; 16 g Carbohydrate; 4 g Fibre; 4 g Protein; 533 mg Sodium

Pictured on page 72 and on back cover.

Safety Tip: Follow manufacturer's instructions for processing hot liquids.

Roasted Garlic Wild Rice Soup

Forget the double, double, toil and trouble. Your cauldron need hardly boil nor bubble.
Once the garlic is roasted, this soup comes together in a snap.

Garlic bulbs	2	2
Canola oil	1 tsp.	5 mL
Chopped onion	1 cup	250 mL
All-purpose flour	1/4 cup	60 mL
Prepared chicken broth	3 cups	750 mL
Water	1 cup	250 mL
Pepper	1/2 tsp.	2 mL
Cooked wild rice (see page 12)	2 cups	500 mL
Grated Parmesan cheese	1/4 cup	60 mL
Chopped fresh basil	2 tbsp.	30 mL

Trim 1/4 inch (6 mm) from garlic bulbs to expose tops of cloves, leaving bulbs intact. Wrap loosely in greased foil. Bake in 375°F (190°C) oven for about 45 minutes until tender. Let stand until cool enough to handle. Squeeze garlic bulbs to remove cloves from peel. Discard peel. Mash cloves with fork. Set aside.

Heat canola oil in large saucepan on medium. Add onion. Cook, uncovered, for 5 to 10 minutes, stirring often, until softened.

Add flour. Heat and stir for 1 minute.

Slowly add 2 cups (500 mL) broth. Heat and stir for about 2 minutes until boiling and thickened. Add remaining broth, water and pepper. Stir. Add roasted garlic. Bring to a boil, stirring constantly with whisk.

Add wild rice. Stir. Cook for about 5 minutes, stirring occasionally, until heated through. Remove from heat.

Add cheese and basil. Stir. Makes about 5 cups (1.25 L).

1 cup (250 mL): 189 Calories; 3.7 g Total Fat (1.4 g Mono, 0.7 g Poly, 1.3 g Sat); 4 mg Cholesterol; 30 g Carbohydrate; 2 g Fibre; 10 g Protein; 565 mg Sodium

Brown Rice Quinoa Pilaf

A hearty, flavourful side gets a flavour and texture twist with the addition of quinoa.
The cranberries add a tangy touch to this nutty yet sweet dish.

Olive (or canola) oil	1 tbsp.	15 mL
Finely chopped onion	1 cup	250 mL
Grated carrot	1 cup	250 mL
Long-grain brown rice	1 cup	250 mL
Prepared chicken broth	3 1/2 cups	875 mL
Quinoa, rinsed and drained	1 cup	250 mL
Dried cranberries	1/2 cup	125 mL

Heat olive oil in large saucepan on medium. Add onion and carrot. Cook, uncovered, for 5 to 10 minutes, stirring often, until onion is softened.

Add rice. Stir until coated. Add broth. Stir. Bring to a boil. Reduce heat to medium-low. Simmer, covered, for 20 minutes, without stirring.

Add quinoa and cranberries. Stir. Bring to a boil. Reduce heat to medium-low. Simmer, covered, for 20 to 25 minutes, without stirring, until rice and quinoa are tender and broth is absorbed. Makes about 7 cups (1.75 L).

1 cup (250 mL): 268 Calories; 5.0 g Total Fat (2.4 g Mono, 1.2 g Poly, 0.8 g Sat); 0 mg Cholesterol; 48 g Carbohydrate; 5 g Fibre; 8 g Protein; 409 mg Sodium

Paré Pointer

The marathon runner's calves hurt, so he went to see a vet.

Millet Cashew Pilaf

Chili and cashews give this dish a star quality that just may take it from sideshow to main attraction!

Canola oil	2 tsp.	10 mL
Millet	1 1/2 cups	375 mL
Chopped onion	1 cup	250 mL
Chopped red pepper	1 cup	250 mL
Chopped celery	1/2 cup	125 mL
Finely grated ginger root	1 tsp.	5 mL
(or 1/4 tsp., 1 mL, ground ginger)		
Garlic clove, minced	1	1
(or 1/4 tsp., 1 mL, powder)		
Prepared chicken broth	3 cups	750 mL
Soy sauce	1 tbsp.	15 mL
Sesame oil (for flavour)	2 tsp.	10 mL
Sweet chili sauce	2 tsp.	10 mL
Can of mandarin orange segments, drained	10 oz.	284 mL
Unsalted, roasted cashews	3/4 cup	175 mL
Grated orange zest	1/2 tsp.	2 mL
Unsalted, roasted sunflower seeds	2 tbsp.	30 mL
Sesame seeds, toasted (see Tip, page 28)	2 tsp.	10 mL

Heat canola oil in large saucepan on medium. Add next 6 ingredients. Cook, uncovered, for about 5 minutes, stirring often, until vegetables are tender-crisp.

Add broth. Stir. Bring to a boil. Reduce heat to medium-low. Simmer, covered, for about 30 minutes, without stirring, until millet is tender and liquid is absorbed.

Combine next 3 ingredients in small cup. Add to millet mixture. Add next 3 ingredients. Stir gently. Transfer to serving dish.

Sprinkle sunflower seeds and sesame seeds over top. Makes about 6 cups (1.5 L).

1 cup (250 mL): 653 Calories; 17.3 g Total Fat (7.6 g Mono, 5.6 g Poly, 3.0 g Sat); 0 mg Cholesterol; 105 g Carbohydrate; 7 g Fibre; 20 g Protein; 655 mg Sodium

Pictured on page 89.

Whole-Grain Gnocchi

Gnocchi (pronounced NOH-kee), an Italian dumpling, is simply delizioso *with a divine pasta sauce, or simply served with butter and Parmesan cheese. (And they freeze well, so you may want to make a double batch!)*

Unpeeled potatoes	1 lb.	454 g
All-purpose flour	1/2 cup	125 mL
Whole-Grain Cereal Blend, page 15	1/4 cup	60 mL
Whole-wheat flour	1/4 cup	60 mL
Grated Parmesan cheese	2 tbsp.	30 mL
Salt	1/4 tsp.	1 mL
Pepper	1/4 tsp.	1 mL
Water	16 cups	4 L
Salt	2 tsp.	10 mL

Prick potatoes in several places with a fork. Wrap individually with paper towels. Microwave on high (100%) for about 10 minutes, turning at halftime, until tender. Let stand until cool enough to handle. Cut potatoes in half lengthwise. Scoop pulp into large bowl. Discard skins. Mash potato pulp.

Add next 6 ingredients. Stir well. Turn out onto lightly floured surface. Knead until smooth. Divide dough into 4 equal portions. Roll portions into 18 inch (45 cm) long ropes, about 1/2 inch (12 mm) thick. Cut ropes into 3/4 inch (2 cm) pieces. Press fork tines into side of each piece. Place pieces on waxed paper-lined baking sheet with sides. Makes about 100 pieces.

Combine water and salt in large pot. Bring to a boil. Add half of gnocchi (see Note). Boil, uncovered, for 2 to 4 minutes until gnocchi float to the top. Transfer with slotted spoon to medium bowl. Repeat with remaining gnocchi. Makes about 3 1/2 cups (875 mL).

1 cup (250 mL): 265 Calories; 2.0 g Total Fat (0.5 g Mono, 0.4 g Poly, 0.9 g Sat); 3 mg Cholesterol; 54 g Carbohydrate; 5 g Fibre; 8 g Protein; 1578 mg Sodium

Note: If you only want to cook a small amount, freeze remaining gnocchi on floured baking sheets for at least 6 hours or overnight. Transfer frozen gnocchi to resealable freezer bag. Cook from frozen.

Wheat Succotash

We've added an extra inducement to this favourite southern side—wheat and a spicy heat. Goes nicely with blackened fish or roast pork.

Canola oil	1 tsp.	5 mL
Chopped onion	1 cup	250 mL
All-purpose flour	1 tbsp.	15 mL
Can of diced tomatoes (with juice)	14 oz.	398 mL
Diced red pepper	1 cup	250 mL
Can of diced green chilies	4 oz.	113 g
Salt	1/2 tsp.	2 mL
Pepper	1/4 tsp.	1 mL
Cooked hard red wheat (see page 10)	1 1/2 cups	375 mL
Frozen (or canned) kernel corn	1 cup	250 mL
Frozen (or canned, rinsed and drained) lima beans	1 cup	250 mL

Heat canola oil in medium saucepan on medium. Add onion. Cook, uncovered, for about 5 minutes, stirring often, until onion starts to soften.

Sprinkle with flour. Heat and stir for 1 minute.

Add next 5 ingredients. Stir. Cook for about 5 minutes, stirring occasionally, until thickened.

Add remaining 3 ingredients. Stir. Cook for about 5 minutes, stirring occasionally, until heated through. Makes about 5 cups (1.25 L).

1 cup (250 mL): 306 Calories; 2.5 g Total Fat (0.8 g Mono, 1.0 g Poly, 0.3 g Sat); 0 mg Cholesterol; 63 g Carbohydrate; 11 g Fibre; 14 g Protein; 554 mg Sodium

Pictured on page 89.

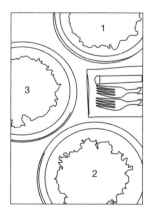

1. Quinoa Salad, page 58
2. Nutty Wild Rice Salad, page 60
3. Tabbouleh, page 57

Props courtesy of: Canadian Tire
The Bay

Curried Fruit Wild Rice

Think wild rice doesn't quite live up to its name? Curry and fruit give this grain some bite—and the vibrant colours add an extra edge.

Canola oil	2 tsp.	10 mL
Finely chopped onion	1 cup	250 mL
Curry powder	2 tsp.	10 mL
Garlic cloves, minced	2	2
(or 1/2 tsp., 2 mL, powder)		
Bay leaf	1	1
Cooked wild rice (see page 12)	3 cups	750 mL
Chopped cooking apple (such as McIntosh)	1 cup	250 mL
Chopped dried apricot	1/2 cup	125 mL
Chopped frozen (or fresh) mango pieces	1/2 cup	125 mL
Evaporated milk	1/2 cup	125 mL
Prepared chicken broth	1/2 cup	125 mL
Dried cranberries	1/4 cup	60 mL
Lemon juice	1/2 tsp.	2 mL

Heat canola oil in large saucepan on medium. Add onion. Cook, uncovered, for about 5 minutes, stirring often, until onion starts to soften.

Add next 3 ingredients. Stir (see Note). Cook for 1 minute.

Add remaining 8 ingredients. Stir. Bring to a boil. Reduce heat to medium-low. Simmer, covered, for 10 minutes, stirring occasionally, to blend flavours. Discard bay leaf. Makes about 6 cups (1.5 L).

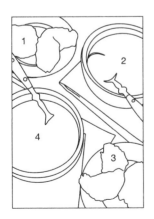

1 cup (250 mL): 206 Calories; 3.8 g Total Fat (1.6 g Mono, 0.8 g Poly, 1.2 g Sat); 6 mg Cholesterol; 40 g Carbohydrate; 4 g Fibre; 6 g Protein; 99 mg Sodium

Note: While stirring, be careful not to break up the bay leaf.

1. Chai, Millet and Rice Biscuits, page 46
2. Spicy Coconut Rice Soup, page 62
3. Savoury Drop Biscuits, page 52
4. Avocado Rice Soup, page 65

Props courtesy of: Pier 1 Imports
Stokes
Canadian Tire
Danesco Inc.
Pfaltzgraff Canada

Bulgur Pear Gratin

Serve your guests this gourmet gratin and their gratitude will know no bounds!
Sophisticated and unexpected, smoky prosciutto and savoury cheeses blend perfectly
with sweet pear and mild fennel.

Canola oil	2 tsp.	10 mL
Thinly sliced onion	2 cups	500 mL
Thinly sliced fennel bulb (white part only)	1 cup	250 mL
Garlic cloves, minced	2	2
(or 1/2 tsp., 2 mL, powder)		
Pepper	1/4 tsp.	1 mL
Thinly sliced peeled pear	2 cups	500 mL
Grated Gruyère cheese	1 cup	250 mL
Chopped prosciutto ham	1/3 cup	75 mL
Dried oregano	1/2 tsp.	2 mL
Dried basil	1/4 tsp.	1 mL
Evaporated milk	1/2 cup	125 mL
Prepared chicken broth	1/2 cup	125 mL
Bulgur	1 cup	250 mL
Fine dry whole-wheat bread crumbs	2/3 cup	150 mL
(see Tip, page 97)		
Grated Parmesan cheese	1/3 cup	75 mL
Butter (or hard margarine), melted	1/4 cup	60 mL

Heat canola oil in large frying pan on medium. Add next 4 ingredients.
Cook for about 5 minutes, stirring often, until onion starts to soften.
Remove from heat. Add pear. Stir. Set aside.

Combine next 4 ingredients in medium bowl. Set aside.

Combine evaporated milk and broth in small bowl.

To assemble, layer ingredients in greased 2 quart (2 L) shallow baking dish
as follows:

1. Half of onion mixture
2. 1/2 cup (125 mL) bulgur
3. Half of prosciutto mixture
4. Remaining onion mixture

(continued on next page)

74 Sides

5. Remaining bulgur
6. Remaining prosciutto mixture
7. Evaporated milk mixture

Combine remaining 3 ingredients in separate small bowl. Sprinkle evenly over top. Cover with greased foil. Bake in 350°F (175°C) oven for 30 minutes. Remove and discard foil. Bake for another 15 minutes until top is golden. Serves 6.

1 serving: 454 Calories; 22.1 g Total Fat (6.5 g Mono, 1.5 g Poly, 11.8 g Sat); 64 mg Cholesterol; 48 g Carbohydrate; 7 g Fibre; 20 g Protein; 767 mg Sodium

Vegetable Quinoa

Veg out while this fresh and easy vegetable dish simmers. Great with grilled fish or chicken.

Canola oil	1 tsp.	5 mL
Chopped green pepper	1/2 cup	125 mL
Chopped onion	1/2 cup	125 mL
Finely chopped celery	1/2 cup	125 mL
Finely chopped carrot	1/4 cup	60 mL
Vegetable cocktail juice	1 1/4 cups	300 mL
Water	3/4 cup	175 mL
Salt	1/4 tsp.	1 mL
Quinoa, rinsed and drained	1 cup	250 mL
Dried dillweed	1/2 tsp.	2 mL
Pepper	1/4 tsp.	1 mL

Heat canola oil in medium saucepan on medium. Add next 4 ingredients. Cook, uncovered, for about 5 minutes, stirring often, until onion is softened.

Add next 3 ingredients. Stir. Bring to a boil. Add quinoa. Stir. Reduce heat to medium-low. Simmer, covered, for about 25 minutes, without stirring, until quinoa is tender and liquid is absorbed. Fluff with fork.

Add dill and pepper. Stir. Makes about 4 cups (1 L).

1 cup (250 mL): 202 Calories; 3.8 g Total Fat (1.3 g Mono, 1.4 g Poly, 0.4 g Sat); 0 mg Cholesterol; 37 g Carbohydrate; 4 g Fibre; 7 g Protein; 378 mg Sodium

Barley Squash Risotto

Risotto without the rice! Barley gives this version a firmer texture that combines perfectly with fresh sage and butternut squash.

Prepared vegetable broth	5 cups	1.25 L
Olive (or canola) oil	2 tbsp.	30 mL
Butter (or hard margarine)	1 tbsp.	15 mL
Sliced leek (white part only)	2 cups	500 mL
Garlic clove, minced	1	1
(or 1/4 tsp., 1 mL, powder)		
Cubed butternut squash	2 cups	500 mL
Pot barley	3/4 cup	175 mL
Dry (or alcohol-free) white wine	1/2 cup	125 mL
Chopped fresh spinach leaves, lightly packed	2 cups	500 mL
Grated Parmesan cheese	2 tbsp.	30 mL
Chopped fresh sage	1 tbsp.	15 mL
(or 3/4 tsp., 4 mL, dried)		

Measure broth into small saucepan. Bring to a boil. Reduce heat to low. Cover to keep hot.

Heat olive oil and butter in large saucepan on medium. Add leek and garlic. Cook, uncovered, for about 5 minutes, stirring often, until leek is softened.

Add squash and barley. Cook for about 5 minutes, stirring occasionally, until squash starts to soften.

Add wine. Cook and stir for about 1 minute until wine is almost absorbed. Add 1 cup (250 mL) hot broth, stirring constantly, until broth is absorbed. Repeat with remaining broth, 1/2 cup (125 mL) at a time, until broth is absorbed and barley is tender. Entire process will take about 50 minutes.

Add spinach. Heat and stir for about 1 minute until spinach is wilted.

Add cheese and sage. Stir. Serve immediately. Makes about 5 1/4 cups (1.3 L).

1 cup (250 mL): 270 Calories; 8.9 g Total Fat (4.6 g Mono, 0.7 g Poly, 2.6 g Sat); 8 mg Cholesterol; 39 g Carbohydrate; 8 g Fibre; 7 g Protein; 540 mg Sodium

Pictured on page 89.

Buckwheat Wild Rice Dressing

Don't just stuff that chicken—dress it up right with a savoury blend of bacon, buckwheat, rice and veggies. This dressing is also designed to go well with pork.

Bacon slices, diced	6	6
Chopped onion	1 cup	250 mL
Finely chopped celery	1 cup	250 mL
Finely chopped fresh white mushrooms	2 cups	500 mL
Prepared chicken broth	1 1/4 cups	300 mL
Finely chopped red pepper	1 cup	250 mL
Whole buckwheat, toasted (see Tip, page 31)	1/2 cup	125 mL
Cajun seasoning	1 tbsp.	15 mL
Garlic cloves, minced (or 1/2 tsp., 2 mL, powder)	2	2
Cooked Wild and Brown Rice Blend, page 13	2 cups	500 mL

Cook bacon in medium frying pan on medium, stirring often, until browned and crisp. Transfer with slotted spoon to paper towel-lined plate to drain. Set aside.

Heat 2 tsp. (10 mL) drippings in same frying pan on medium. Add onion and celery. Cook for about 5 minutes, stirring often, until onion starts to soften.

Add mushrooms. Cook for about 5 minutes, stirring occasionally, until mushrooms start to brown.

Add next 5 ingredients and bacon. Stir. Bring to a boil. Reduce heat to medium-low. Simmer, covered, for about 15 minutes, without stirring, until buckwheat is tender and broth is absorbed.

Add rice blend. Cook and stir for about 5 minutes until heated through. Makes about 5 1/2 cups (1.4 L).

1 cup (250 mL): 194 Calories; 5.8 g Total Fat (2.4 g Mono, 1.0 g Poly, 1.9 g Sat); 9 mg Cholesterol; 28 g Carbohydrate; 3 g Fibre; 9 g Protein; 715 mg Sodium

Broccoli Cheese Barley

Flavour and texture contrasts abound in this hearty casserole—firm barley, crisp broccoli, crunchy almonds and creamy cheese. Makes the perfect potluck offering.

Butter (or hard margarine)	1 tbsp.	15 mL
Chopped onion	1 cup	250 mL
All-purpose flour	2 1/2 tbsp.	37 mL
Milk	2 1/2 cups	625 mL
Lemon pepper	1 tsp.	5 mL
Grated sharp Cheddar cheese	1 1/2 cups	375 mL
Cooked pot barley (see page 11)	3 3/4 cups	925 mL
Frozen chopped broccoli, thawed	2 1/2 cups	625 mL
Fine dry whole-wheat bread crumbs (see Tip, page 97)	3 tbsp.	50 mL
Sliced almonds	2 tbsp.	30 mL
Cooking spray		

Melt butter in large saucepan on medium. Add onion. Cook, uncovered, for about 10 minutes, stirring often, until soft.

Sprinkle with flour. Heat and stir for 1 minute.

Slowly add milk, stirring constantly, until smooth. Heat and stir for about 5 minutes until boiling and thickened. Remove from heat.

Add lemon pepper and cheese. Stir until melted.

Add barley and broccoli. Mix well. Spread evenly in greased 2 quart (2 L) shallow baking dish.

Combine bread crumbs and almonds in small bowl. Sprinkle over top. Lightly spray crumb mixture with cooking spray. Bake, uncovered, in 400°F (205°C) oven for about 25 minutes until golden. Makes about 7 cups (1.75 L).

1 cup (250 mL): 566 Calories; 13.6 g Total Fat (1.3 g Mono, 0.4 g Poly, 6.9 g Sat); 29 mg Cholesterol; 88 g Carbohydrate; 19 g Fibre; 24 g Protein; 271 mg Sodium

 tip Hot peppers contain capsaicin in the seeds and ribs. Removing the seeds and ribs will reduce the heat. Wear rubber gloves when handling hot peppers and avoid touching your eyes. Wash your hands well afterwards.

Coconut Vegetable Curry

With coconut milk instead of cream, vegetable broth instead of chicken broth, and lots of fresh vegetables and spices, everyone will forget they're eating something good for them!

Can of light coconut milk	14 oz.	398 mL
Prepared vegetable broth	1 cup	250 mL
Granulated sugar	3 tbsp.	50 mL
Soy sauce	3 tbsp.	50 mL
Lime juice	2 tbsp.	30 mL
Red curry paste	1 tsp.	5 mL
Can of chickpeas (garbanzo beans), rinsed and drained	19 oz.	540 mL
Can of cut baby corn, drained	14 oz.	398 mL
Chopped onion	1 cup	250 mL
Sliced carrot	1 cup	250 mL
Sliced celery	1 cup	250 mL
Pot barley	1/2 cup	125 mL
Chopped fresh asparagus	1 cup	250 mL
Chopped red pepper	1 cup	250 mL

Whisk first 6 ingredients in medium bowl until smooth.

Put next 6 ingredients in 3 1/2 to 4 quart (3.5 to 4 L) slow cooker. Pour coconut milk mixture over top. Stir. Cook, covered, on Low for 8 to 9 hours or on High for 4 to 4 1/2 hours.

Add asparagus and red pepper. Cook, covered, on High for 20 to 30 minutes until asparagus and red pepper are tender-crisp. Makes about 8 cups (2 L).

1 cup (250 mL): 287 Calories; 6.1 g Total Fat (0.6 g Mono, 1.2 g Poly, 3.1 g Sat); 0 mg Cholesterol; 51 g Carbohydrate; 8 g Fibre; 11 g Protein; 782 mg Sodium

Stuffed Acorn Squash

Tired of tacos? Bored with burritos? Stuff this spicy meat and grain mixture into a tender, sweet squash instead.

Acorn squash	2	2
Canola oil	2 tsp.	10 mL
Chopped onion	1 cup	250 mL
Lean ground beef	1/2 lb.	225 g
Finely chopped fresh white mushrooms	2 cups	500 mL
Garlic cloves, minced	2	2
(or 1/2 tsp., 2 mL, powder)		
All-purpose flour	2 tbsp.	30 mL
Diced Roma (plum) tomato	1 cup	250 mL
Ketchup	1/4 cup	60 mL
Finely chopped fresh jalapeño pepper	1 tbsp.	15 mL
(see Tip, page 78)		
Chili powder	2 tsp.	10 mL
Ground cumin	1 tsp.	5 mL
Salt	1/2 tsp.	2 mL
Pepper	1/4 tsp.	1 mL
Cooked millet (see page 11)	1 cup	250 mL
Cooked Wild and Brown	1 cup	250 mL
Rice Blend, page 13		
Frozen (or canned) kernel corn, thawed	1 cup	250 mL

Cut squash in half lengthwise. Remove seeds. Place, cut-side down, on greased baking sheet with sides. Bake in 350°F (175°C) oven for about 40 minutes until tender when pierced with a fork.

Heat canola oil in large frying pan on medium. Add onion. Cook for about 5 minutes, stirring often, until starting to soften.

Add beef. Scramble-fry for about 5 minutes until no longer pink. Drain.

Add mushrooms and garlic. Cook for about 5 minutes, stirring occasionally, until mushrooms start to turn brown.

Sprinkle with flour. Heat and stir for 2 minutes. Add next 7 ingredients. Cook for 2 to 3 minutes, stirring occasionally, until thickened.

Add remaining 3 ingredients. Stir. Cook for about 1 minute until heated through. Fill squash halves with rice mixture. Makes 4 stuffed squash halves.

(continued on next page)

Pictured on page 90.

Wheat Wild Rice Meatloaf

Is your usual meatloaf a little tame? Add wild rice and some exotic Asian flavours and your meatloaf will have everyone's stomach growling.

Canola oil	2 tsp.	10 mL
Finely chopped onion	1 cup	250 mL
Finely chopped celery	1/2 cup	125 mL
Finely chopped red pepper	1/2 cup	125 mL
Grated carrot	1/2 cup	125 mL
Garlic cloves, minced (or 1/2 tsp., 2 mL, powder)	2	2
Cooked hard red wheat (see Tip, page 33)	1 cup	250 mL
Cooked wild rice (see Tip, page 33)	1 cup	250 mL
Large eggs	2	2
Balsamic vinegar	1/3 cup	75 mL
Orange juice	1/3 cup	75 mL
Maple (or maple-flavoured) syrup	2 tbsp.	30 mL
Soy sauce	2 tbsp.	30 mL
Chili paste (sambal oelek)	2 tsp.	10 mL
Sesame oil (for flavour)	2 tsp.	10 mL
Lean ground beef	1 lb.	454 g
Lean ground pork	1 lb.	454 g

Heat canola oil in large frying pan on medium. Add onion. Cook for about 5 minutes, stirring often, until starting to soften. Add next 4 ingredients. Cook for about 5 minutes, stirring occasionally, until carrot is tender-crisp. Transfer to medium bowl.

Add wheat and wild rice. Stir well.

Whisk next 7 ingredients in large bowl. Add beef and pork. Mix well. Add wheat mixture. Press into greased 9 x 5 x 3 inch (22 x 12.5 x 7.5 cm) loaf pan. Bake, uncovered, in 375°F (190°C) oven for about 80 minutes until fully cooked and internal temperature reaches 160°F (71°C). Let stand for 10 minutes. Cut into slices. Serves 8.

Wild Porcupine Meatballs

Hear the kids squeal with delight when you present them with hearty porcupine meatballs for dinner (for fun, tell them the rice grains are quills). The tomato sauce makes this the perfect topper for pasta.

Water	1 1/2 cups	375 mL
Salt	1/8 tsp.	0.5 mL
Wild rice	1/2 cup	125 mL
Large egg, fork-beaten	1	1
Fine dry whole-wheat bread crumbs (see Tip, page 97)	1/4 cup	60 mL
Finely chopped onion	1/4 cup	60 mL
Cajun seasoning	1 tsp.	5 mL
Lean ground beef	1 lb.	454 g
Canola oil	1 tsp.	5 mL
Chopped onion	1 cup	250 mL
Garlic clove, minced (or 1/2 tsp., 2 mL, powder)	2	2
Can of diced tomatoes (with juice)	28 oz.	796 mL
Prepared beef broth	1 cup	250 mL
Can of tomato sauce	7 1/2 oz.	213 mL
Granulated sugar	1 tsp.	5 mL
Dried basil	1/2 tsp.	2 mL
Dried oregano	1/2 tsp.	2 mL
Salt	1/4 tsp.	1 mL

Measure water and salt into Dutch oven. Bring to a boil. Add wild rice. Stir. Reduce heat to medium-low. Simmer, covered, for about 30 minutes, without stirring, until wild rice starts to soften. Drain. Let stand, uncovered, for 10 minutes.

Combine next 4 ingredients in large bowl. Add beef and wild rice. Mix well. Roll into 1 inch (2.5 cm) balls. Makes about 40 meatballs. Set aside.

Heat canola oil in same Dutch oven on medium. Add onion and garlic. Cook for about 5 minutes, stirring often, until onion starts to soften.

Add remaining 7 ingredients. Stir. Bring to a boil. Add meatballs. Stir. Reduce heat to medium. Boil gently, covered, for about 1 hour, stirring occasionally, until rice is tender but chewy and internal temperature of beef reaches 160°F (71°C). Makes about 6 cups (1.5 L).

(continued on next page)

1 cup (250 mL): 294 Calories; 12.5 g Total Fat (5.6 g Mono, 0.8 g Poly, 4.6 g Sat); 76 mg Cholesterol; 26 g Carbohydrate; 2 g Fibre; 21 g Protein; 979 mg Sodium

Bulgur Stir-Fry

The addition of bulgur to this saucy, raspberry-flavoured stir-fry adds a whole new flavour experience.

Soy sauce	2 tbsp.	30 mL
Cornstarch	1 tsp.	5 mL
Sweet chili sauce	3 tbsp.	50 mL
Raspberry vinegar	2 tbsp.	30 mL
Dijon mustard	1 tsp.	5 mL
Sesame oil (for flavour)	1 tsp.	5 mL
Beef top sirloin steak, cut into 1/8 inch (3 mm) strips	1 lb.	454 g
Canola oil	1 tsp.	5 mL
Canola oil	1 tsp.	5 mL
Thinly sliced onion	1 cup	250 mL
Sugar snap peas, trimmed	2 1/2 cups	625 mL
Thinly sliced red pepper	1 cup	250 mL
Fresh asparagus, trimmed of tough ends and cut into 2 inch (5 cm) pieces	1/2 lb.	225 g
Cooked bulgur (see page 9)	2 cups	500 mL

Stir soy sauce into cornstarch in small cup. Add next 3 ingredients. Stir. Set aside.

Pour sesame oil over beef in medium bowl. Stir. Heat wok or large frying pan on medium-high until very hot. Add first amount of canola oil. Add beef. Stir-fry for 2 to 3 minutes until no longer pink. Transfer to small bowl. Cover to keep warm.

Add second amount of canola oil to hot wok. Add onion. Stir-fry for 2 minutes. Add next 3 ingredients. Stir-fry for about 3 minutes until vegetables are tender-crisp. Stir cornstarch mixture. Add to vegetable mixture. Heat and stir until boiling and thickened.

Add bulgur and beef. Cook and stir until heated through. Makes about 8 cups (2 L).

1 cup (250 mL): 219 Calories; 9.1 g Total Fat (4.0 g Mono, 1.0 g Poly, 3.1 g Sat); 27 mg Cholesterol; 19 g Carbohydrate; 4 g Fibre; 16 g Protein; 501 mg Sodium

Wheat Crepes Cannelloni

Es-crepe from the ordinary entree. Dressed in a creamy Parmesan sauce, tender little rolls with a beef, spinach and wheat filling are unique—and tasty! If you're watching your salt intake, use a lower-sodium pasta sauce and broth.

WHEAT CREPES

Large eggs	3	3
Water	1 cup	250 mL
Salt	1/2 tsp.	2 mL
All-purpose flour	2/3 cup	150 mL
Whole-wheat flour	2/3 cup	150 mL

PARMESAN CREAM SAUCE

Butter (or hard margarine)	1/4 cup	60 mL
All-purpose flour	2 tbsp.	30 mL
Whole-wheat flour	2 tbsp.	30 mL
Milk	1 cup	250 mL
Prepared beef broth	1 cup	250 mL
Grated Parmesan cheese	1/2 cup	125 mL

FILLING

Canola oil	1 tsp.	5 mL
Lean ground beef	1/2 lb.	225 g
Chopped onion	1 cup	250 mL
Garlic clove, minced (or 1/4 tsp., 1 mL, powder)	1	1
Box of frozen chopped spinach, thawed and squeezed dry	10 oz.	300 g
Soaked cracked wheat (see Note)	2/3 cup	150 mL
Dried oregano	1 tsp.	5 mL
Dried sage	1/2 tsp.	2 mL
Pepper	1/2 tsp.	2 mL
Tomato pasta sauce	3 cups	750 mL

Chopped fresh parsley, for garnish

(continued on next page)

Wheat Crepes: Whisk first 3 ingredients in medium bowl until combined. Slowly add all-purpose and whole-wheat flour, stirring constantly with whisk, until smooth. Let stand for 30 minutes. Stir. Heat medium non-stick frying pan on medium. Spray with cooking spray. Pour 1/4 cup (60 mL) batter into pan. Immediately swirl batter to coat bottom, lifting and tilting pan to ensure entire bottom is covered. Cook for about 15 seconds until top is set and bottom is lightly golden. Turn crepe over. Cook for about 15 seconds until brown spots appear on bottom. Remove to plate. Repeat with remaining batter, spraying pan with cooking spray if necessary to prevent sticking. Makes about 8 crepes.

Parmesan Cream Sauce: Melt butter in small saucepan on medium. Add all-purpose and whole-wheat flour. Heat and stir for 1 minute. Slowly add milk and broth, stirring constantly with whisk, until smooth. Heat and stir until boiling and thickened. Remove from heat.

Add cheese. Stir. Cover to keep warm. Makes about 2 1/3 cups (575 mL) sauce.

Filling: Heat canola oil in large frying pan on medium. Add next 3 ingredients. Scramble-fry for about 5 minutes until beef is no longer pink. Drain.

Add next 5 ingredients. Cook for 5 minutes, stirring occasionally. Add 1 cup (250 mL) Parmesan Cream Sauce. Stir well. Let stand until cool.

Spread 1 cup (250 mL) pasta sauce in 9 x 13 inch (22 x 33 cm) baking dish. Spoon about 1/2 cup (125 mL) beef mixture down centre of each crepe. Roll to enclose filling. Arrange filled crepes over pasta sauce. Spoon remaining pasta sauce over crepes. Drizzle remaining Parmesan Cream Sauce over top. Bake, uncovered, in 350°F (175°C) oven for about 45 minutes until sauce is bubbling. Let stand for 5 minutes.

Garnish with parsley. Serves 4.

1 serving: 713 Calories; 30.1 g Total Fat (10.1 g Mono, 2.2 g Poly, 14.6 g Sat); 216 mg Cholesterol; 77 g Carbohydrate; 12 g Fibre; 37 g Protein; 2084 mg Sodium

Pictured on page 90.

Note: To make 2/3 cup (150 mL) cooked cracked wheat, pour 1/2 cup (125 mL) boiling water over 1/4 cup (60 mL) cracked wheat in small heatproof bowl. Let stand, covered, for 5 minutes. Drain.

Bulgur Beef Koftas

This take on the traditional Middle Eastern meatball will have your belly dancing (with joy) in no time. Try substituting ground lamb for ground beef for a more authentic variation.

Prepared beef broth	1 cup	250 mL
Bulgur	1/2 cup	125 mL
Lean ground beef	3/4 lb.	340 g
Finely chopped onion	1/2 cup	125 mL
Garlic cloves, minced	2	2
(or 1/2 tsp., 2 mL, powder)		
Ground coriander	1/2 tsp.	2 mL
Ground cumin	1/2 tsp.	2 mL
Ground allspice	1/4 tsp.	1 mL
Large egg	1	1
Fine dry whole-wheat bread crumbs	1/2 cup	125 mL
(see Tip, page 97)		
Chopped fresh cilantro or parsley	2 tbsp.	30 mL
(or 1 1/2 tsp., 7 mL, dried)		
Chopped fresh mint	2 tbsp.	30 mL
(or 1 1/2 tsp., 7 mL, dried)		
Salt	1/2 tsp.	2 mL
Pepper	1/2 tsp.	2 mL
Bamboo skewers (8 inches, 20 cm, each),	12	12
soaked in water for 10 minutes		
Canola oil	1 tbsp.	15 mL

Combine broth and bulgur in small saucepan. Bring to a boil. Remove from heat. Let stand for about 30 minutes until bulgur is tender and broth is absorbed.

Put next 6 ingredients and bulgur into food processor. Process until mixture forms a coarse paste.

Add next 6 ingredients. Process until combined. Transfer to medium bowl. Divide bulgur mixture into 24 equal portions. Shape into egg-sized oval patties.

(continued on next page)

Entrees - Beef

Press 2 patties around each skewer. Arrange skewers on greased baking sheet with sides. Brush skewers with canola oil. Broil on top rack in oven for 4 to 5 minutes per side until fully cooked and internal temperature of beef reaches 160°F (71°C). Makes 12 skewers.

1 skewer: 112 Calories; 5.8 g Total Fat (2.7 g Mono, 0.6 g Poly, 1.8 g Sat); 32 mg Cholesterol; 8 g Carbohydrate; 1 g Fibre; 8 g Protein; 213 mg Sodium

---

Beef and Beer Stew

The beer connoisseur will be glad to know that this hearty beef, beer and barley stew goes marvellously well with...beer! (The gravy thickens after standing.)

Pot barley	1/2 cup	125 mL
Thinly sliced onion	1 cup	250 mL
Chopped carrot	1 cup	250 mL
Chopped celery	1 cup	250 mL
Garlic cloves, minced	2	2
(or 1/2 tsp., 2 mL, powder)		
Canola oil	2 tsp.	10 mL
Stewing beef, trimmed of fat	2 lbs.	900 g
Bottle of brown ale or stout	14 oz.	398 mL
Prepared beef broth	1 cup	250 mL
Water	1 cup	250 mL
Brown sugar, packed	2 tbsp.	30 mL
Dijon mustard	1 tbsp.	15 mL
Chili powder	2 tsp.	10 mL
Dried thyme	1/2 tsp.	2 mL
Salt	1/2 tsp.	2 mL
Pepper	1/4 tsp.	1 mL
Chopped fresh parsley (optional)	2 tbsp.	30 mL

Layer first 5 ingredients, in order given, in 4 to 5 quart (4 to 5 L) slow cooker.

Heat canola oil in large frying pan on medium-high. Cook beef, in 2 batches, for 3 to 5 minutes, stirring occasionally, until browned. Transfer to slow cooker.

Combine next 9 ingredients in same frying pan. Heat and stir, scraping any brown bits from bottom of pan, until boiling. Add to slow cooker. Cook, covered, on Low for 8 to 9 hours or on High for 4 to 4 1/2 hours.

Sprinkle with parsley. Makes about 7 1/2 cups (1.9 L).

1 cup (250 mL): 290 Calories; 10.1 g Total Fat (4.4 g Mono, 0.7 g Poly, 3.3 g Sat); 75 mg Cholesterol; 20 g Carbohydrate; 3 g Fibre; 26 g Protein; 375 mg Sodium

Everyday Baked Chicken

Switching from fried chicken to baked doesn't have to be a sacrifice when it's double-coated for extra crunch! Take the skin off the drumsticks if you're opting for a more heart-healthy choice.

Large flake rolled oats	1 1/4 cups	300 mL
Grated Parmesan cheese	2 tbsp.	30 mL
Ground flaxseed (see Tip, page 49)	2 tbsp.	30 mL
Taco seasoning	2 tbsp.	30 mL
Yellow cornmeal	2 tbsp.	30 mL
Sesame seeds	1 tbsp.	15 mL
Pepper	1/4 tsp.	1 mL
Dried oregano	1 tsp.	5 mL
Egg whites (large)	3	3
Chicken drumsticks (3 – 5 oz., 85 – 140 g, each)	12	12

Cooking spray

Process first 8 ingredients in food processor or blender for about 15 seconds until mixture is powdered. Transfer to large resealable freezer bag.

Beat egg whites in medium shallow bowl until frothy. Add 4 drumsticks to oat mixture. Toss until coated. Dip coated drumsticks into egg whites. Return to oat mixture. Toss until coated. Arrange on greased baking sheet with sides. Repeat with remaining drumsticks, oat mixture and egg whites. Discard any remaining oat mixture and egg whites.

Spray chicken with cooking spray. Bake in 375°F (190°C) oven for about 50 minutes, turning at halftime, until golden brown and internal temperature reaches 170°F (77°C). Makes 12 drumsticks.

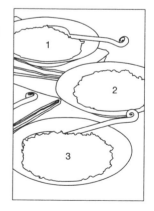

1 drumstick: 160 Calories; 5.9 g Total Fat (1.8 g Mono, 1.5 g Poly, 1.5 g Sat); 66 mg Cholesterol; 7 g Carbohydrate; 1 g Fibre; 19 g Protein; 158 mg Sodium

1. Barley Squash Risotto, page 76
2. Wheat Succotash, page 70
3. Millet Cashew Pilaf, page 68

Props courtesy of: Pier 1 Imports
Stokes
Canadian Tire

Cajun Chicken and Barley

Try this spicy tomato and barley dish and see for yourself what all the fuss is about.

Boneless, skinless chicken thighs, halved	1 1/4 lbs.	560 g
Canola oil	1 tsp.	5 mL
Hot Italian sausage, casing removed, chopped	1/2 lb.	225 g
Can of diced tomatoes (with juice)	14 oz.	398 mL
Chopped green pepper	1 1/2 cups	375 mL
Chopped celery	1 cup	250 mL
Chopped onion	1 cup	250 mL
Prepared chicken broth	1 cup	250 mL
Can of tomato sauce	7 1/2 oz.	213 mL
Pot barley	1/2 cup	125 mL
Cajun seasoning	2 tsp.	10 mL
Garlic cloves, minced (or 1/2 tsp., 2 mL, powder)	2	2

Put chicken into 3 1/2 to 4 quart (3.5 to 4 L) slow cooker.

Heat canola oil in medium frying pan on medium. Add sausage. Scramble-fry for about 5 minutes until starting to brown. Transfer with slotted spoon to paper towel-lined plate to drain.

Combine remaining 9 ingredients in large bowl. Pour over chicken. Add sausage. Stir well. Cook, covered, on Low for 7 to 8 hours or on High for 3 1/2 to 4 hours until barley is tender. Makes about 9 cups (2.25 L).

1 cup (250 mL): 248 Calories; 12.2 g Total Fat (5.2 g Mono, 2.1 g Poly, 3.7 g Sat); 61 mg Cholesterol; 15 g Carbohydrate; 3 g Fibre; 19 g Protein; 753 mg Sodium

Pictured on page 125.

1. Stuffed Acorn Squash, page 80
2. Wheat Crepes Cannelloni, page 84
3. Stuffed Pork Tenderloin, page 112

Props courtesy of: Pier 1 Imports
Winners Stores

Baked Spring Rolls

Just as crisp as the fried variety, with lots of added whole-grain goodness.

Prepared chicken broth	1 cup	250 mL
Millet	1/4 cup	60 mL
Quinoa, rinsed and drained	1/4 cup	60 mL
Canola oil	2 tsp.	10 mL
Lean ground chicken	1/2 lb.	225 g
Canola oil	1 tsp.	5 mL
Finely chopped onion	1 cup	250 mL
Julienned carrot (see Tip, page 93)	1 cup	250 mL
Julienned bamboo shoots (see Tip, page 93)	1 cup	250 mL
Thinly sliced fresh shiitake mushrooms	1/2 cup	125 mL
Soy sauce	2 tbsp.	30 mL
Finely grated ginger root (or 3/4 tsp., 4 mL, ground ginger)	1 tbsp.	15 mL
Garlic cloves, minced (or 1/2 tsp., 2 mL, powder)	2	2
Chili paste (sambal oelek)	1 – 2 tsp.	5 – 10 mL
Hoisin sauce	1 tsp.	15 mL
Phyllo pastry sheets, thawed according to package directions	16	16
Cooking spray		

Measure broth into small saucepan. Bring to a boil. Add millet and quinoa. Stir. Reduce heat to medium-low. Simmer, covered, for about 30 minutes, without stirring, until millet and quinoa are tender and broth is absorbed. Transfer to large bowl. Fluff with fork.

Heat first amount of canola oil in large frying pan on medium-high. Add chicken. Scramble-fry for about 5 minutes until no longer pink. Add to millet mixture. Stir.

Heat second amount of canola oil in same frying pan on medium. Add onion and carrot. Cook for about 5 minutes, stirring often, until onion starts to soften.

(continued on next page)

Add next 7 ingredients. Cook and stir for about 5 minutes until liquid is evaporated. Add to millet mixture. Stir.

Place 1 pastry sheet on work surface with longest side closest to you. Cover remaining sheets with damp towel to prevent drying. Spray sheet with cooking spray. Place second sheet on top. Spray with cooking spray. Fold in half crosswise. Spray with cooking spray. Place about 1/2 cup (125 mL) millet mixture across bottom of sheet, leaving 1 inch (2.5 cm) border on each side. Fold sides over filling. Roll up from bottom to enclose filling. Brush edge with water to seal. Place, seam-side down, on greased baking sheet with sides. Cover rolls with separate damp towel to prevent drying. Repeat with remaining pastry sheets and grain mixture.

Spray rolls with cooking spray. Bake in 375°F (190°C) oven for about 25 minutes until browned. Makes 8 spring rolls.

1 spring roll: 303 Calories; 10.1 g Total Fat (3.1 g Mono, 1.7 g Poly, 1.0 g Sat); trace Cholesterol; 41 g Carbohydrate; 3 g Fibre; 12 g Protein; 653 mg Sodium

Pictured on page 107.

 To julienne, cut into very thin strips that resemble matchsticks.

Quick Chicken Quinoa Stew

Does waiting around for hours for stew to simmer get you stewing mad? Well, if patience is not your virtue, this is the stew for you. Serve with crusty bread.

Olive (or cooking) oil	2 tsp.	10 mL
Boneless, skinless chicken thighs (about 3 oz., 85 g, each)	6	6
Chopped celery	1 cup	250 mL
Chopped onion	1 cup	250 mL
Chopped red pepper	1 cup	250 mL
Garlic cloves, minced (or 1/2 tsp., 2 mL, powder)	2	2
Can of plum tomatoes (with juice)	28 oz.	796 mL
Prepared chicken broth	2 cups	500 mL
Chopped sun-dried tomatoes in oil, blotted dry	1/4 cup	60 mL
Tomato paste (see Tip, page 113)	3 tbsp.	50 mL
Dried basil	1 tsp.	5 mL
Dried crushed chilies	1/2 tsp.	2 mL
Dried oregano	1/2 tsp.	2 mL
Salt	1 tsp.	5 mL
Pepper	1/4 tsp.	1 mL
Dried rosemary, crushed	1/8 tsp.	0.5 mL
Quinoa, rinsed and drained	2/3 cup	150 mL

Heat olive oil in Dutch oven on medium-high. Add chicken. Cook, uncovered, for 2 to 3 minutes per side until browned. Remove to plate. Set aside. Reduce heat to medium.

Add celery and onion to same pot. Cook for about 5 minutes, stirring often, until onion starts to soften. Add red pepper and garlic. Cook for 1 minute, stirring occasionally.

Add next 10 ingredients. Stir. Cook for about 5 minutes, stirring occasionally and breaking up tomatoes, until boiling.

Add quinoa and chicken. Reduce heat to medium-low. Simmer, covered, for about 30 minutes until chicken is fully cooked and quinoa is tender. Serves 6.

1 serving: 298 Calories; 10.4 g Total Fat (4.4 g Mono, 2.3 g Poly, 2.4 g Sat); 57 mg Cholesterol; 29 g Carbohydrate; 5 g Fibre; 22 g Protein; 1089 mg Sodium

Chicken Couscous Cakes

Full of hearty chicken, rice and veggies, these colourful chicken patties certainly take the cake!

Whole wheat couscous	1/4 cup	60 mL
Boiling water	1/2 cup	125 mL
Canola oil	1 tsp.	5 mL
Finely chopped onion	1 cup	250 mL
Finely chopped red pepper	1 cup	250 mL
Chopped cooked chicken	2 cups	500 mL
Cooked wild rice (see page 12)	1 cup	250 mL
Fine dry whole-wheat bread crumbs (see Tip, page 97)	1/2 cup	125 mL
Garlic and herb no-salt seasoning	1 tbsp.	15 mL
Large egg, fork-beaten	1	1
Grated jalapeño Monterey Jack cheese	1/2 cup	125 mL

Cooking spray

Measure couscous into small heatproof bowl. Add boiling water. Stir. Let stand, covered, for about 5 minutes until liquid is absorbed. Fluff with fork. Set aside.

Heat canola oil in large frying pan on medium. Add onion and red pepper. Cook for about 5 minutes, stirring often, until onion starts to soften. Transfer to large bowl.

Add next 4 ingredients and couscous. Stir.

Add egg and cheese. Mix well. Divide into 12 equal portions. Shape into 3 inch (7.5 cm) diameter cakes. Arrange on greased baking sheet with sides.

Spray cakes with cooking spray. Bake in 375°F (190°C) oven for about 20 minutes until firm. Makes 12 cakes.

1 cake: 109 Calories; 4.2 g Total Fat (1.5 g Mono, 0.7 g Poly, 1.5 g Sat); 37 mg Cholesterol; 9 g Carbohydrate; 1 g Fibre; 9 g Protein; 74 mg Sodium

Pictured on page 126.

Italian Rice Cups

Let your cup runneth over—with chicken, sausage, herbs and bubbly melted cheese. Invert the cups onto a plate so you and your guests can see the luscious, golden-brown Parmesan cheese crust.

Large eggs, fork-beaten	2	2
Cooked Wild and Brown Rice Blend, page 13	2 cups	500 mL
Cooked millet (see page 11)	1 cup	250 mL
Grated Parmesan cheese	1/2 cup	125 mL
Canola oil	2 tsp.	10 mL
Lean ground chicken	3/4 lb.	340 g
Hot Italian sausage, casing removed (about 3 oz., 85 g)	1	1
Finely chopped onion	1 cup	250 mL
Finely chopped celery	1/2 cup	125 mL
Finely chopped red pepper	1/2 cup	125 mL
Tomato sauce	1/2 cup	125 mL
Chili sauce	1 tbsp.	15 mL
Garlic cloves, minced (or 1/2 tsp., 2 mL, powder)	2	2
Dried basil	1/2 tsp.	2 mL
Dried oregano	1/2 tsp.	2 mL
Grated mozzarella cheese	1 cup	250 mL

Combine first 4 ingredients in medium bowl. Set aside.

Heat canola oil in large frying pan on medium-high. Add chicken and sausage. Scramble-fry for about 5 minutes until no longer pink. Add onion and celery. Cook for about 3 minutes, stirring often, until onion starts to soften.

Add next 6 ingredients. Stir. Cook for 1 minute. Press 1/3 cup (75 mL) rice mixture firmly into bottom and up sides of 6 well-greased 6 oz. (170 mL) custard cups or ramekins. Place about 1/2 cup (125 mL) chicken mixture in centre of each cup. Press remaining rice mixture on top of chicken mixture.

(continued on next page)

Sprinkle mozzarella cheese over top. Pour 1/2 inch (12 mm) hot water into 9 x 13 inch (22 x 33 cm) pan. Place cups in pan. Bake in 375°F (190°C) oven for 30 minutes. Transfer cups from pan to wire rack. Let stand for 5 minutes. Run knife around edges of cups to loosen. Makes 6 rice cups.

1 rice cup: 358 Calories; 22.5 g Total Fat (5.7 g Mono, 1.7 g Poly, 6.5 g Sat); 95 mg Cholesterol; 15 g Carbohydrate; 2 g Fibre; 23 g Protein; 530 mg Sodium

Pictured on page 126.

 To make dry whole-wheat bread crumbs, remove the crusts from slices of stale or two-day-old whole-wheat bread. Leave the bread on the counter for a day or two until it's dry, or, if you're in a hurry, set the bread slices on a baking sheet and bake in a 200°F (95°C) oven, turning occasionally, until dry. Break the bread into pieces and process until crumbs reach the desired fineness. One slice of bread will make about 1/4 cup (60 mL) fine dry breadcrumbs. Freeze extra bread crumbs in an airtight container or in a resealable freezer bag.

Shrimp Rice Skillet

A spicy-sweet medley of shrimp and sweet fruit, tossed in a tangy peanut sauce.
Loved by young and old alike!

Salsa	1/4 cup	60 mL
Honey	2 tbsp.	30 mL
Lime juice	2 tbsp.	30 mL
Low-sodium soy sauce	2 tbsp.	30 mL
Smooth peanut butter	2 tbsp.	30 mL
Canola oil	1 tbsp.	15 mL
Chopped red pepper	1 cup	250 mL
Chopped green onion	1/2 cup	125 mL
Garlic clove, minced	1	1
(or 1/4 tsp., 1 mL, powder)		
Cooked long-grain brown rice	2 cups	500 mL
(see page 10)		
Uncooked medium shrimp	1/2 lb.	225 g
(peeled and deveined)		
Salt	1/4 tsp.	1 mL
Pepper	1/4 tsp.	1 mL
Fresh bean sprouts	2 cups	500 mL
Can of pineapple chunks, drained	14 oz.	398 mL
Chopped frozen (or fresh)	1 cup	250 mL
mango pieces, thawed		
Dry-roasted peanuts	1/2 cup	125 mL

Combine first 5 ingredients in small microwave-safe cup. Microwave on high (100%) for about 20 seconds until peanut butter is softened. Stir until smooth. Set aside.

Heat large frying pan on medium-high until very hot. Add canola oil. Add next 3 ingredients. Stir-fry for 2 minutes.

Add next 4 ingredients. Stir-fry for about 2 minutes until shrimp start to turn pink.

(continued on next page)

Add remaining 4 ingredients. Stir-fry for 1 to 2 minutes until heated through. Microwave peanut butter mixture on high (100%) for about 15 seconds until warm. Pour over rice mixture. Toss until coated. Serve immediately. Makes about 6 cups (1.5 L).

1 cup (250 mL): 341 Calories; 12.6 g Total Fat (6.0 g Mono, 3.9 g Poly, 1.9 g Sat); 57 mg Cholesterol; 45 g Carbohydrate; 5 g Fibre; 16 g Protein; 366 mg Sodium

Pictured on page 125.

Salmon Amaranth Bake

Wow your guests with an exotic grain, and with the fresh flavours of salmon and lemon. But little will they know that with a flick of a food processor switch your meal was already half made!

Salmon fillets, skin removed, cut up	1 lb.	454 g
Large egg	1	1
Cooked amaranth (see Tip, page 33)	1/2 cup	125 mL
Fine dry whole-wheat bread crumbs (see Tip, page 97)	1/2 cup	125 mL
Soy sauce	1 tbsp.	15 mL
Grated lemon zest	2 tsp.	10 mL
Salt	1/4 tsp.	1 mL
Pepper	1/2 tsp.	2 mL
SAUCE		
Mayonnaise	1/2 cup	125 mL
Sour cream	1/4 cup	60 mL
Chopped fresh basil	1 tbsp.	15 mL
Lemon juice	1 tsp.	5 mL

Process first 8 ingredients in food processor until almost smooth. Spread evenly in greased 9 inch (22 cm) round pan. Bake, uncovered, in 375°F (190°C) oven for about 20 minutes until firm and golden.

Sauce: Combine all 4 ingredients in small bowl. Spread half of sauce over salmon mixture. Serve remaining sauce on the side. Serves 4.

1 serving: 539 Calories; 35.4 g Total Fat (16.6 g Mono, 11.4 g Poly, 5.7 g Sat); 131 mg Cholesterol; 25 g Carbohydrate; 3 g Fibre; 30 g Protein; 770 mg Sodium

Salmon Cabbage Rolls

This tasty twist on tradition uses salmon and pot barley as tantalizing additions to the standard rice filling. We'd certainly swim upstream for it!

Prepared chicken broth	4 cups	1 L
Long-grain brown rice	2/3 cup	150 mL
Pot barley	1/3 cup	75 mL
Wild rice	1/3 cup	75 mL
Large head of green cabbage	1	1
Boiling water, to cover		
Canola oil	1 tsp.	5 mL
Diced onion	1/2 cup	125 mL
Chopped fresh dill	2 tbsp.	30 mL
(or 1 1/2 tsp., 7 mL, dried)		
Grated lemon zest	1 tsp.	5 mL
Salt, sprinkle		
Pepper, sprinkle		
Cans of red (or pink) salmon, drained,	2	2
skin and round bones removed		
(7 1/2 oz., 213 g, each), see Note 1		
ONION CREAM SAUCE		
Canola oil	1/2 tsp.	2 mL
Chopped onion	1/4 cup	60 mL
Garlic clove, minced	1	1
(or 1/4 tsp., 1 mL, powder)		
All-purpose flour	2 tbsp.	30 mL
Skim evaporated milk	3/4 cup	175 mL
Milk	1/2 cup	125 mL
Grated lemon zest	1/2 tsp.	2 mL
Chopped fresh dill	2 tsp.	10 mL
(or 1/2 tsp., 2 mL, dried)		

Measure broth into large saucepan. Bring to a boil. Add next 3 ingredients. Stir. Reduce heat to medium-low. Simmer, covered, for about 45 minutes until almost tender. Drain, reserving 1 1/3 cups (325 mL) broth. Set aside.

(continued on next page)

Remove core from cabbage. Trim about 1/2 inch (12 mm) slice from bottom. Place, cut-side down, in Dutch oven or large pot. Cover with boiling water. Cover Dutch oven with foil. Let stand for 5 minutes. Drain. Let stand until cool enough to handle. Carefully remove 12 large outer leaves from cabbage. Cut "V" shape along tough ribs of leaves to remove. Discard ribs. Set leaves aside. Remove another 6 leaves from cabbage. Chop. Spread evenly in ungreased 9 x 13 inch (22 x 33 cm) baking dish (see Note 2). Set aside.

Heat canola oil in small frying pan on medium. Add onion. Cook for about 5 minutes, stirring often, until softened.

Add next 4 ingredients. Heat and stir for about 1 minute until fragrant.

Flake salmon with fork in large bowl. Add onion mixture and rice mixture. Toss gently. Place about 1/3 cup (75 mL) salmon mixture on 1 cabbage leaf. Fold in sides. Roll up tightly from bottom to enclose filling. Repeat with remaining salmon mixture and cabbage leaves. Arrange cabbage rolls, seam-side down, over chopped cabbage. Pour reserved broth over cabbage rolls. Cover with foil. Bake in 350°F (175°C) oven for about 1 1/2 hours until cabbage is softened.

Onion Cream Sauce: Heat canola oil in small saucepan on medium. Add onion and garlic. Cook for about 5 minutes, stirring often, until onion is softened.

Sprinkle with flour. Heat and stir for 1 minute. Slowly add evaporated milk and milk, stirring constantly, until smooth. Heat and stir for 5 to 10 minutes until boiling and thickened. Remove from heat.

Add lemon zest and fresh dill. Stir. Makes about 1 cup (250 mL) sauce. Drizzle over cabbage rolls. Makes 12 cabbage rolls. Serves 6.

1 serving: 363 Calories; 10.7 g Total Fat (1.1 g Mono, 0.8 g Poly, 2.2 g Sat); 47 mg Cholesterol; 44 g Carbohydrate; 6 g Fibre; 25 g Protein; 554 mg Sodium

Note 1: If you have leftover cooked salmon, use about 11 oz. (310 g) instead of canned salmon.

Note 2: Discard any other outer leaves that are partially steamed. Save the remaining cabbage in the refrigerator for another use.

Brown Rice Risotto

Maybe traditional Italian nonnas liked to stand for hours stirring their risotto, but we prefer to pamper those tootsies and stir only when necessary.

Olive oil	2 tbsp.	30 mL
Shallots (or green onions), finely chopped	2	2
Chopped portobello mushrooms	3 cups	750 mL
Finely chopped fresh white mushrooms	1 cup	250 mL
Garlic cloves, minced (or 1/2 tsp., 2 mL, powder)	2	2
Long-grain brown rice	1 cup	250 mL
Dried thyme	1/4 tsp.	1 mL
Prepared chicken broth	2 1/2 cups	625 mL
Dry (or alcohol-free) white wine	1/2 cup	125 mL
Chopped fresh asparagus	2 cups	500 mL
Small bay scallops	1 cup	250 mL
Salt	1/4 tsp.	1 mL
Pepper	1/4 tsp.	1 mL
Lemon juice	1 tbsp.	15 mL
Chopped fresh parsley	2 tbsp.	30 mL

Heat olive oil in large saucepan on medium. Add shallots. Cook for 3 to 5 minutes, stirring occasionally, until tender.

Add next 3 ingredients. Cook for about 5 minutes, stirring occasionally, until liquid is evaporated. Add rice and thyme. Stir.

Add broth and wine. Stir. Bring to a boil. Reduce heat to medium-low. Simmer, covered, for about 45 minutes, without stirring, until rice is tender.

Add asparagus. Stir. Cook, covered, for about 3 minutes until asparagus is tender-crisp. Add next 3 ingredients. Stir. Cook, covered, for about 2 minutes until scallops are opaque.

Add lemon juice. Stir. Sprinkle parsley over top. Makes about 5 1/2 cups (1.4 L).

1 cup (250 mL): 248 Calories; 7.0 g Total Fat (4.3 g Mono, 1.0 g Poly, 1.1 g Sat); 10 mg Cholesterol; 31 g Carbohydrate; 3 g Fibre; 12 g Protein; 517 mg Sodium

Salmon Quinoa Frittata

Don't fritter your time away fretting over dinner. Fix this flavourful frittata and fascinate yourself with the finer things in life. Serve with a salad or fresh vegetables.

Canola oil	1 tbsp.	15 mL
Salmon fillet, skin removed, cut into thin strips	3/4 lb.	340 g
Large eggs	7	7
Milk	1/4 cup	60 mL
Maple (or maple-flavoured) syrup	2 tbsp.	30 mL
Dijon mustard	2 tsp.	10 mL
Salt	1/4 tsp.	1 mL
Cooked quinoa (see page 11)	1 1/2 cups	375 mL
Fine dry whole-wheat bread crumbs (see Tip, page 97)	2/3 cup	150 mL
Grated mozzarella cheese	1/3 cup	75 mL

Chopped fresh parsley, for garnish

Heat canola oil in large frying pan on medium. Arrange salmon in single layer in frying pan.

Whisk next 5 ingredients in medium bowl until smooth. Add quinoa and bread crumbs. Stir. Pour over salmon. Reduce heat to medium-low. Cook, covered, for about 15 minutes until bottom is golden and top is almost set. Remove from heat.

Sprinkle cheese over top. Broil on centre rack in oven (see Tip, below) for about 5 minutes until cheese is melted and golden.

Garnish with parsley. Cuts into 8 wedges.

1 wedge: 239 Calories; 11.0 g Total Fat (4.3 g Mono, 2.4 g Poly, 2.6 g Sat); 190 mg Cholesterol; 17 g Carbohydrate; 1 g Fibre; 18 g Protein; 236 mg Sodium

 tip   When baking or broiling food in a frying pan with a handle that isn't ovenproof, wrap the handle in tin foil and keep it to the front of the oven, away from the element.

Curry Fish Pie

Curry the favour of all those you feed by currying the flavour of this delightful, savoury pie. A slightly sweet, crunchy oat crust is filled with a curry-scented egg mixture accented with sweet peppers and flavourful fish pieces. This crust can be used with savoury and sweet fillings alike.

Bulgur	3 tbsp.	50 mL
Chopped dried apricot	3 tbsp.	50 mL
Boiling water	1/3 cup	75 mL
CRUST		
Large flake rolled oats	3/4 cup	175 mL
Whole-wheat flour	1/2 cup	125 mL
Butter (or hard margarine), softened	1/3 cup	75 mL
Ground walnuts	1/4 cup	60 mL
Maple (or maple-flavoured) syrup	2 tbsp.	30 mL
FILLING		
Curry powder	1 1/2 tsp.	7 mL
Salt	1/4 tsp.	1 mL
Pepper	1/8 tsp.	0.5 mL
Halibut (or other firm white fish), any small bones removed, cut into 1 inch (2.5 cm) pieces	1/2 lb.	225 g
Canola oil	1 tbsp.	15 mL
Chopped onion	1/2 cup	125 mL
Finely chopped red pepper	1/2 cup	125 mL
Garlic clove, minced (or 1/4 tsp., 1 mL, powder)	1	1
Grated Gruyère cheese	1 cup	125 mL
Large eggs	3	3
Milk	3/4 cup	175 mL
Curry powder	1/2 tsp.	2 mL
Ground cumin	1/8 tsp.	0.5 mL
Salt	1/2 tsp.	2 mL
Pepper	1/4 tsp.	1 mL

(continued on next page)

Combine bulgur and apricot in small heatproof bowl. Add boiling water. Stir. Let stand, covered, for 15 minutes. Fluff with fork. Set aside.

Crust: Mix first 4 ingredients in medium bowl until mixture resembles coarse crumbs. Add syrup. Stir until moistened. Mixture will be like cookie dough. Press into bottom and up side of greased 9 inch (22 cm) deep dish pie plate. Bake in 375°F (190°C) oven for about 10 minutes until set. Set aside. Reduce heat to 350°F (175°C).

Filling: Combine first 3 ingredients in large resealable freezer bag. Add fish. Toss until coated. Remove to plate. Discard any remaining seasoning mixture.

Heat canola oil in large frying pan on medium. Add onion. Cook for about 5 minutes, stirring often, until onion starts to soften. Add red pepper, garlic and bulgur mixture. Heat and stir for 2 minutes. Remove from heat. Let stand for 10 minutes.

Sprinkle cheese over crust. Spread bulgur mixture over cheese. Arrange fish over top.

Whisk remaining 6 ingredients in medium bowl until combined. Pour over fish. Bake, uncovered, for about 50 minutes until set and knife inserted in centre comes out clean. Let stand for 10 minutes. Cuts into 6 wedges.

1 wedge: 435 Calories; 25.8 g Total Fat (7.8 g Mono, 4.8 g Poly, 11.3 g Sat); 152 mg Cholesterol; 30 g Carbohydrate; 4 g Fibre; 22 g Protein; 494 mg Sodium

Pictured on page 107.

Paré Pointer
She thought you had to go to the top of a mountain to see the mountaineers.

Tuna-Stuffed Tomatoes

*With its medley of tuna, herbs and vegetables, this delightful dish will bring
a harmony of fresh flavours to your dinner table.*

Large tomatoes	6	6
Cooked long-grain brown rice (see page 10)	1 1/2 cups	375 mL
Can of flaked white (or light) tuna in water, drained	6 oz.	170 g
Large hard-cooked eggs, chopped	2	2
Grated zucchini (with peel)	1/2 cup	125 mL
Finely chopped celery	1/4 cup	60 mL
Thinly sliced green onion	1/4 cup	60 mL
Chopped fresh basil (or 1 1/2 tsp., 7 mL, dried)	2 tbsp.	30 mL
Chopped fresh mint (or 3/4 tsp., 4 mL, dried)	1 tbsp.	15 mL
Grated lemon zest	1 tsp.	5 mL
Salt	1 tsp.	5 mL
Pepper	1/2 tsp.	2 mL

Trim 1/2 inch (12 mm) slice from top of each tomato. Using small spoon,
scoop out seeds from each tomato. Discard seeds. Scoop out pulp. Chop
pulp and tomato tops. Put into large bowl.

Add remaining 11 ingredients. Stir. Spoon rice mixture into tomato cups.
Makes 6 stuffed tomatoes.

*1 stuffed tomato: 154 Calories; 3.5 g Total Fat (1.2 g Mono,
0.9 g Poly, 0.9 g Sat); 84 mg Cholesterol; 20 g Carbohydrate;
3 g Fibre; 12 g Protein; 442 mg Sodium*

Pictured at right.

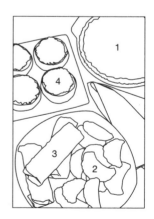

1. Curry Fish Pie, page 104
2. Kasha Pastries, page 122
3. Baked Spring Rolls, page 92
4. Tuna-Stuffed Tomatoes, above

Props courtesy of: Pier 1 Imports
Canadian Tire

Barley Pecan Sole

Stick it to those frozen battered fish sticks! These barley and pecan-crusted sole fillets are sure to please the whole family.

Barley flour	2/3 cup	150 mL
Finely chopped pecans	1/3 cup	75 mL
Large flake rolled oats	1/3 cup	75 mL
Chopped fresh dill	2 tbsp.	30 mL
(or 1 1/2 tsp., 7 mL, dried)		
Garlic powder	1 1/4 tsp.	6 mL
Paprika	1 1/4 tsp.	6 mL
Salt	1/4 tsp.	1 mL
Sole fillets, any small bones removed	1 1/2 lbs.	680 g
Cooking spray		
Lemon wedges, for garnish	6	6

Combine first 7 ingredients in medium shallow bowl.

Press both sides of fillets into flour mixture until coated. Arrange in single layer on greased baking sheet with sides. Spray fillets with cooking spray. Bake in 375°F (190°C) oven for about 10 minutes until fish flakes easily when tested with fork. Transfer to serving plate.

Garnish with lemon wedges. Serves 6.

1 serving: 224 Calories; 6.6 g Total Fat (3.0 g Mono, 2.1 g Poly, 0.9 g Sat); 54 mg Cholesterol; 17 g Carbohydrate; 3 g Fibre; 25 g Protein; 191 mg Sodium

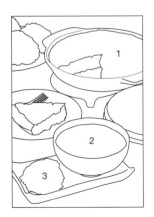

1. Savoury Blue Cheese Tart, page 121
2. Chicken Millet Chowder, page 64
3. Cornmeal Pepper Lime Scones, page 47

Props courtesy of: Stokes
Pier 1 Imports
Linens N' Things
The Bay
Out of the Fire Studio

Bulgur Lamb Stew

Your guests will surely flock to the table for a taste of this sweet and spicy Moroccan stew.

All-purpose flour	1/4 cup	60 mL
Ground cinnamon	1 tsp.	5 mL
Ground ginger	1 tsp.	5 mL
Ground cumin	1/2 tsp.	2 mL
Salt	1/2 tsp.	2 mL
Pepper	1/4 tsp.	1 mL
Stewing lamb, trimmed of fat	1 1/2 lbs.	680 g
Canola oil	2 tbsp.	30 mL
Chopped onion	1 1/2 cups	375 mL
Chopped red pepper	1 1/2 cups	375 mL
Prepared chicken broth	1 1/2 cups	375 mL
Dry (or alcohol-free) white wine	3/4 cup	175 mL
Honey	3 tbsp.	50 mL
Finely grated ginger root	1 tbsp.	15 mL
(or 3/4 tsp., 4 mL, ground ginger)		
Garlic cloves, minced	3	3
(or 3/4 tsp., 4 mL, powder)		
Lemon juice	1 tbsp.	15 mL
Salt	1/2 tsp.	2 mL
Pepper	1/2 tsp	2 mL
Bulgur	1 cup	250 mL
Raisins	1 cup	250 mL
Chopped dried apricot	2/3 cup	150 mL
Pitted prunes	1/2 cup	125 mL

Combine first 6 ingredients in large resealable freezer bag. Add lamb. Toss until coated. Discard any remaining flour mixture.

Heat canola oil in Dutch oven on medium-high. Add lamb. Cook, uncovered, for about 5 minutes, stirring occasionally, until browned.

(continued on next page)

Add onion and red pepper. Cook for about 3 minutes, stirring often, until onion starts to soften.

Add next 8 ingredients. Heat and stir, scraping any brown bits from bottom of pot, until boiling. Remove from heat. Bake, covered, in 300°F (150°C) oven for 1 hour (see Note).

Add remaining 4 ingredients. Stir. Bake, covered, for another 30 minutes until lamb is tender and liquid is absorbed. Makes about 7 cups (1.75 L).

1 cup (250 mL): 456 Calories; 9.9 g Total Fat (4.5 g Mono, 1.9 g Poly, 2.3 g Sat); 63 mg Cholesterol; 65 g Carbohydrate; 5 g Fibre; 25 g Protein; 499 mg Sodium

Note: If your Dutch oven doesn't have heatproof handles, wrap the handles in foil before baking.

Paré Pointer

He thought the stock market was where you sold cattle.

Stuffed Pork Tenderloin

Buckwheat and spice, and apricot so nice, that's what a good pork tenderloin is made of.

Canola oil	1 tsp.	5 mL
Finely chopped celery	1/4 cup	60 mL
Finely chopped onion	1/4 cup	60 mL
Garlic clove, minced	1	1
(or 1/4 tsp., 1 mL, powder)		
Prepared beef broth	1 cup	250 mL
Chopped dried apricot	1/2 cup	125 mL
Whole buckwheat	1/3 cup	75 mL
Dried thyme	1/2 tsp.	2 mL
Salt	1/2 tsp.	2 mL
Pepper	1/4 tsp.	1 mL
Cooked wild rice (see page 12)	1/2 cup	125 mL
Chopped fresh parsley	1 tbsp.	15 mL
(or 3/4 tsp., 4 mL, flakes)		
Pork tenderloin, trimmed of fat	1 lb.	454 g
Canola oil	1 tsp.	5 mL

Heat canola oil in medium saucepan on medium. Add next 3 ingredients. Cook for about 2 minutes, stirring often, until celery and onion start to soften.

Add next 6 ingredients. Stir. Bring to a boil. Reduce heat to medium-low. Simmer, covered, for about 15 minutes, without stirring, until buckwheat is tender and broth is absorbed. Add wild rice and parsley. Stir.

To butterfly pork, cut horizontally lengthwise almost, but not quite through, to other side. Open flat. Place between 2 sheets of plastic wrap. Pound with mallet or rolling pin to 7 x 11 inch (18 x 28 cm) rectangle. Spoon buckwheat mixture lengthwise along centre of tenderloin. Press buckwheat mixture so it holds together. Roll up tightly, starting from long edge to enclose filling. Tie with butcher's string.

(continued on next page)

Heat second amount of canola oil in large frying pan on medium-high. Add pork roll. Cook for about 5 minutes, turning occasionally, until browned on all sides. Transfer to greased wire rack set in baking sheet with sides. Bake in 375°F (190°C) oven for about 30 minutes until internal temperature reaches 160°F (71°C). Remove to platter. Cover with foil. Let stand for 10 minutes. Remove and discard butcher's string. Cut into slices. Serves 4.

1 serving: 268 Calories; 5.7 g Total Fat (2.8 g Mono, 1.1 g Poly, 1.3 g Sat); 67 mg Cholesterol; 24 g Carbohydrate; 3 g Fibre; 30 g Protein; 565 mg Sodium

Pictured on page 90.

 If a recipe calls for less than an entire can of tomato paste, freeze the unopened can for 30 minutes. Open both ends and push the contents through one end. Slice off only what you need. Freeze the remaining paste in a resealable freezer bag or plastic wrap for future use.

Lamb Moussaka

A traditional Greek casserole with flavourful layers of lamb, eggplant and cheese sauce. We dare your guests to go home hungry!

Medium eggplants (with peel), cut lengthwise into 1/4 inch (6 mm) slices	2	2
Salt	1 tsp.	5 mL
Canola oil	2 tsp.	10 mL
LAMB MEAT SAUCE		
Canola oil	2 tsp.	10 mL
Lean ground lamb	1 lb.	454 g
Chopped onion	2 cups	500 mL
Garlic cloves, minced (or 1 tsp., 5 mL, powder)	4	4
Can of stewed tomatoes	19 oz.	540 mL
Dry (or alcohol-free) red wine	1 cup	250 mL
Tomato paste (see Tip, page 113)	1/4 cup	60 mL
Dried oregano	2 tsp.	10 mL
Ground cinnamon	1 tsp.	5 mL
Salt	1 1/2 tsp.	7 mL
Pepper	1/2 tsp.	2 mL
Millet	1/2 cup	125 mL
Cooked wild rice (see page 12)	2 cups	500 mL
Chopped fresh parsley (or 3 1/2 tsp., 17 mL, flakes)	1/3 cup	75 mL
WHITE CHEESE SAUCE		
All-purpose flour	6 tbsp.	100 mL
Ground nutmeg	1/4 tsp.	1 mL
Salt	1/4 tsp.	1 mL
Pepper	1/4 tsp.	1 mL
Milk	2 cups	500 mL
Large eggs	4	4
Ricotta cheese	2 cups	500 mL
Crumbled feta cheese	1/2 cup	125 mL

(continued on next page)

Sprinkle both sides of eggplant slices with salt. Place on wire rack set in baking sheet with sides. Let stand for 20 minutes. Rinse with cold water. Blot dry with paper towels. Arrange in single layer on greased baking sheet with sides.

Brush eggplant slices with canola oil. Broil on top rack in oven for about 5 minutes per side until golden. Set aside.

Lamb Meat Sauce: Heat canola oil in Dutch oven or large pot on medium-high. Add lamb. Scramble-fry for about 5 minutes until no longer pink.

Add onion and garlic. Cook, uncovered, for 5 to 10 minutes, stirring often, until onion starts to brown. Reduce heat to medium.

Add next 7 ingredients. Stir. Bring to a boil. Add millet. Stir. Reduce heat to medium-low. Cook, covered, for about 30 minutes until thickened and millet is tender.

Add wild rice and parsley. Stir. Makes about 5 1/2 cups (1.4 L) meat sauce.

White Cheese Sauce: Combine first 4 ingredients in medium saucepan on medium. Slowly add milk, stirring constantly with whisk, until smooth. Heat and stir for 8 to 10 minutes until boiling and thickened. Remove from heat.

Whisk remaining 3 ingredients in medium bowl until combined. Add to milk mixture. Stir. Makes about 5 cups (1.25 L) cheese sauce.

To assemble, layer ingredients in greased 9 x 13 inch (22 x 33 cm) baking dish as follows:

1. Half meat sauce
2. 1/3 cheese sauce
3. Half eggplant slices, slightly overlapping
4. Remaining meat sauce
5. 1/3 cheese sauce
6. Remaining eggplant slices, slightly overlapping
7. Remaining cheese sauce

Bake, uncovered, in 350°F (175°C) oven for 65 to 70 minutes until top is browned and bubbly. Let stand for 10 minutes before serving. Serves 8.

1 serving: 650 Calories; 30.3 g Total Fat (10.9 g Mono, 3.2 g Poly, 13.9 g Sat); 177 mg Cholesterol; 59 g Carbohydrate; 7 g Fibre; 31 g Protein; 1231 mg Sodium

Pictured on page 125.

Wheat Calzone

This Naples staple fits the bill when you want pizza taste but can do without the whole pie. Personalize the filling with the flavours you wish to savour.

CRUST

All-purpose flour	1 cup	250 mL
Whole-wheat flour	3/4 cup	175 mL
Baking powder	2 tsp.	10 mL
Granulated sugar	2 tsp.	10 mL
Baking soda	1 tsp.	5 mL
Salt	1/2 tsp.	2 mL
Buttermilk (or soured milk, see Tip, page 38)	2/3 cup	150 mL
Canola oil	2 tbsp.	30 mL
Fancy (mild) molasses	1 tbsp.	15 mL

FILLING

Boiling water	3 tbsp.	50 mL
Bulgur	2 tbsp.	30 mL
Pizza sauce	1/2 cup	125 mL
Diced deli ham	1 cup	250 mL
Grated mozzarella cheese	2 cups	500 mL

Crust: Measure first 6 ingredients into large bowl. Stir. Make a well in centre.

Combine next 3 ingredients in small bowl. Add to well. Stir until soft dough forms. Turn out onto lightly floured surface. Knead 8 times.

Filling: Combine boiling water and bulgur in small heatproof bowl. Let stand for about 20 minutes until bulgur is softened.

Add remaining 3 ingredients. Stir. Divide dough into 4 equal portions. Shape portions into balls. Roll out 1 portion to form an 8 inch (20 cm) diameter circle. Place about 2/3 cup (150 mL) filling on half of circle, leaving 1 inch (2.5 cm) edge. Fold dough in half over filling. Press edges to seal. Carefully transfer to greased baking sheet. Cut 2 small slits in top to allow steam to escape. Repeat with remaining dough portions and filling. Bake in 425°F (220°C) oven for about 15 minutes until golden. Makes 4 calzones.

1 calzone: 545 Calories; 24.1 g Total Fat (10.2 g Mono, 3.1 g Poly, 9.6 g Sat); 67 mg Cholesterol; 57 g Carbohydrate; 6 g Fibre; 26 g Protein; 1558 mg Sodium

Pictured on page 53.

(continued on next page)

Variation: Use the crust for pizza too! Press dough into greased 12 inch (30 cm) pizza pan. Top with your favourite sauce and toppings. Bake in 425°F (220°C) oven for about 10 minutes until crust is golden. Cuts into 8 wedges.

Sweet Curry Rice

If you like your curry fruity, this is the one for you! Pineapple and honey add character to this flavourful pork and rice dish.

Canola oil	1 tbsp.	15 mL
Boneless fast-fry pork chops, trimmed of fat and cut crosswise into thin strips	1 1/2 lbs.	680 g
Chopped onion	1 1/2 cups	375 mL
Chopped celery	1 cup	250 mL
Long-grain brown rice	1 cup	250 mL
Curry powder	1 tbsp.	15 mL
Garlic cloves, minced (or 1/2 tsp., 2 mL, powder)	2	2
Prepared chicken broth	2 cups	500 mL
Can of crushed pineapple (with juice)	14 oz.	398 mL
Chopped tomato	1 cup	250 mL
Liquid honey	2 tbsp.	30 mL
Salt	1/4 tsp.	1 mL

Heat canola oil in Dutch oven on medium-high. Add pork. Cook, uncovered, for about 5 minutes, stirring occasionally, until no longer pink. Remove to plate. Set aside.

Add onion and celery to same pot. Cook for about 5 minutes, stirring often, until onion starts to soften.

Add next 3 ingredients. Heat and stir for 1 to 2 minutes until fragrant.

Add broth. Stir. Bring to a boil. Reduce heat to medium-low. Simmer, covered, for about 45 minutes, without stirring, until rice is tender.

Add remaining 4 ingredients and pork. Stir. Increase heat to medium. Cook, covered, for about 15 minutes until heated through. Makes about 8 cups (2 L).

1 cup (250 mL): 304 Calories; 10.4 g Total Fat (4.7 g Mono, 1.5 g Poly, 3.1 g Sat); 45 mg Cholesterol; 34 g Carbohydrate; 3 g Fibre; 18 g Protein; 332 mg Sodium

Mushroom Veggie Burgers

The most fabulous bistro in town couldn't dream up something as chicly unique as these moist and tender patties flavoured with leek and cashews.

Cracked wheat	1/2 cup	125 mL
Bulgur	1/3 cup	75 mL
Salt	1/2 tsp.	2 mL
Boiling water	1 1/2 cups	375 mL
Canola oil	1 tbsp.	15 mL
Chopped fresh white mushrooms	3 cups	750 mL
Finely chopped onion	1 cup	250 mL
Finely chopped celery	1/4 cup	60 mL
Finely chopped leek (white part only)	1/4 cup	60 mL
Garlic clove, minced (or 1/4 tsp., 1 mL, powder)	1	1
Raw cashews	1/2 cup	125 mL
Large egg	1	1
Fine dry whole-wheat bread crumbs (see Tip, page 97)	1 cup	250 mL
Salt	1/2 tsp.	2 mL
Pepper	1/4 tsp.	1 mL

Cooking spray

Combine first 3 ingredients in medium heatproof bowl. Add boiling water. Stir. Let stand, covered, for about 30 minutes until bulgur and wheat are tender. Drain well. Transfer to large bowl.

Heat canola oil in large frying pan on medium. Add next 5 ingredients. Cook for about 15 minutes, stirring occasionally, until vegetables start to brown and liquid is evaporated. Spread vegetables on large plate. Cool to room temperature.

Process cashews in food processor until finely chopped.

(continued on next page)

Add next 4 ingredients, bulgur mixture and vegetables. Process with on/off motion until combined. Mixture should still be coarse. Transfer to same large bowl. Divide into 6 equal portions. Shape into 4 inch (10 cm) diameter patties.

Place patties on greased baking sheet with sides. Spray with cooking spray. Broil on centre rack in oven for 5 minutes. Turn patties over. Spray with cooking spray. Broil for another 5 minutes until browned. Makes 6 patties.

1 patty: 190 Calories; 5.7 g Total Fat (2.8 g Mono, 1.4 g Poly, 0.9 g Sat); 31 mg Cholesterol; 30 g Carbohydrate; 5 g Fibre; 7 g Protein; 393 mg Sodium

Paré Pointer

Little Johnny took band-aids to the card game for when they cut the deck.

Spinach Millet Patties

Ever wonder what really goes into a veggie burger? Well, we've spilled the beans—or the millet in this case. Packed with the flavours of feta, oregano, sun-dried tomato and spinach, this patty is a cut above the rest.

Prepared vegetable broth	1 3/4 cups	425 mL
Salt	1/4 tsp.	1 mL
Millet	3/4 cup	175 mL
Canola oil	2 tsp.	10 mL
Chopped onion	1 1/2 cups	375 mL
Chopped fresh spinach leaves, lightly packed	4 cups	1 L
Sun-dried tomato pesto	2 tbsp.	30 mL
Large egg, fork-beaten	1	1
Fine dry whole-wheat bread crumbs (see Tip, page 97)	1 cup	250 mL
Crumbled feta cheese	3/4 cup	175 mL
Dried oregano	1/2 tsp.	2 mL
Pepper	1/2 tsp.	2 mL
Canola oil	1 tbsp.	15 mL

Measure broth and salt into small saucepan. Bring to a boil. Add millet. Stir. Reduce heat to medium-low. Simmer, covered, for about 30 minutes, without stirring, until millet is tender and broth is absorbed. Transfer to large bowl. Cool.

Heat first amount of canola oil in large frying pan on medium. Add onion. Cook for 5 to 10 minutes, stirring often, until softened. Add spinach and pesto. Cook for about 2 minutes, stirring occasionally, until spinach is wilted. Add to millet.

Add next 5 ingredients. Mix well. Divide into 6 equal portions. Using wet hands, press into 3/4 inch (2 cm) thick patties.

Heat second amount of canola oil in same frying pan on medium. Cook patties, in 2 batches, for 4 to 5 minutes per side until browned. Makes 6 patties.

1 patty: 412 Calories; 12.7 g Total Fat (4.8 g Mono, 2.7 g Poly, 4.1 g Sat); 48 mg Cholesterol; 62 g Carbohydrate; 6 g Fibre; 14 g Protein; 619 mg Sodium

Savoury Blue Cheese Tart

Hungry for quiche but not the extra calories? This easy-to-make tart will nicely fill the gap. Wild rice, asparagus and tangy blue cheese make this dish a flavour sensation.

Canola oil	1 tsp.	5 mL
Fresh asparagus tips (3 inch, 7.5 cm, length)	12	12
Chopped fresh asparagus	1 cup	250 mL
Cooked wild rice (see Tip, page 33)	1 cup	250 mL
Grated mozzarella cheese	3/4 cup	175 mL
Crumbled blue cheese	1/4 cup	60 mL
Large eggs, fork-beaten	3	3
Milk	1 1/3 cups	325 mL
Chopped fresh parsley	3 tbsp.	50 mL
(or 2 1/4 tsp., 11 mL, flakes)		
Whole-wheat flour	3/4 cup	175 mL
Baking powder	1 tsp.	5 mL
Salt	1/4 tsp.	1 mL
Pepper	1/4 tsp.	1 mL

Heat canola oil in medium frying pan on medium. Add asparagus tips and chopped asparagus. Cook, covered, for 1 to 2 minutes until bright green. Remove tips to plate. Set aside.

Add rice to frying pan. Stir. Spread evenly in greased 9 inch (22 cm) deep dish pie plate. Sprinkle both cheeses over top.

Combine next 3 ingredients in large bowl.

Combine remaining 4 ingredients in small bowl. Add to egg mixture. Stir well. Pour over asparagus mixture. Arrange asparagus tips in spoke pattern over egg mixture. Bake, uncovered, in 400°F (205°C) oven for about 35 minutes until golden and knife inserted in centre comes out clean. Let stand for 5 minutes. Cuts into 6 wedges.

1 wedge: 219 Calories; 9.1 g Total Fat (3.1 g Mono, 1.0 g Poly, 4.3 g Sat); 111 mg Cholesterol; 23 g Carbohydrate; 3 g Fibre; 13 g Protein; 336 mg Sodium

Pictured on page 108.

Kasha Pastries

Kasha, a traditional Eastern European buckwheat porridge, becomes a main course contender or an appealing appetizer when it's wrapped in flaky pastry.

FILLING

Butter (or hard margarine)	1 tbsp.	15 mL
Finely chopped onion	1/2 cup	125 mL
Garlic clove, minced (or 1/4 tsp., 1 mL, powder)	1	1
Chopped fresh white mushrooms	1 cup	250 mL
Prepared vegetable broth	3/4 cup	175 mL
Finely chopped red pepper	1/4 cup	60 mL
Raisins	1/4 cup	60 mL
Whole buckwheat	1/4 cup	60 mL
Chili powder	1/4 tsp.	1 mL
Ground cinnamon	1/8 tsp.	0.5 mL
Ground cumin	1/8 tsp.	0.5 mL
Salt	1/8 tsp.	0.5 mL
Pepper	1/8 tsp.	0.5 mL

PASTRY

Whole-wheat flour	1 1/2 cups	375 mL
Cold butter (or hard margarine), cut up	1/2 cup	125 mL
Ice water	1/4 cup	60 mL
Large egg	1	1
Water	1 tbsp.	15 mL

Filling: Melt butter in medium saucepan or large frying pan on medium. Add onion and garlic. Cook for 5 to 10 minutes, stirring often, until onion is soft and golden.

Add mushrooms. Cook for about 5 minutes, stirring occasionally, until mushrooms are starting to turn golden.

Add next 9 ingredients. Stir. Bring to a boil. Reduce heat to medium-low. Cook, covered, for about 30 minutes, without stirring, until buckwheat is tender and liquid is absorbed. Transfer to large bowl. Fluff with fork. Chill.

(continued on next page)

Pastry: Measure flour into medium bowl. Cut in butter until mixture resembles coarse crumbs. Add ice water, 1 tbsp. (15 mL) at a time, stirring with fork until mixture starts to come together. Do not over mix. Shape into slightly flattened disc. Wrap with plastic wrap. Chill for 20 minutes. Roll out pastry on lightly floured surface to about 1/8 inch (3 mm) thickness. Cut out circles with 3 inch (7.5 cm) round cookie cutter. Place about 1 tbsp. (15 mL) filling in centre of each circle.

Whisk egg and water in small bowl. Brush edges of pastry with egg mixture. Fold pastry over filling. Press edges together with fork to seal. Cut small vents in tops to allow steam to escape. Place pastries on greased baking sheet with sides. Brush with egg mixture. Bake in 375°F (190°C) oven for about 20 minutes until golden brown. Makes about 20 pastries.

1 pastry: 95 Calories; 5.7 g Total Fat (1.5 g Mono, 0.3 g Poly, 3.4 g Sat); 23 mg Cholesterol; 10 g Carbohydrate; 1 g Fibre; 2 g Protein; 82 mg Sodium

Pictured on page 107.

Paré Pointer

A robot's excuse for not performing right? Usually a screw loose.

Barley Bean Rolls

These crispy, pinwheel burritos are a perfect high-energy snack. Dip in sour cream and salsa.

Can of refried beans	14 oz.	398 mL
Whole-wheat flour tortillas (7 1/2 inch, 19 cm, diameter)	6	6
Cooked pot barley (see Tip, page 33)	2 cups	500 mL
Grated mozzarella and Cheddar cheese blend	3/4 cup	175 mL
Finely chopped pickled jalapeño pepper	1 tbsp.	15 mL
Cooking spray		
Paprika, sprinkle		

Spread about 1/4 cup (60 mL) refried beans on each tortilla, leaving 1 inch (2.5 cm) edge.

Combine next 3 ingredients in medium bowl. Sprinkle over refried beans. Roll up tightly, jelly-roll style. Secure each roll with 2 wooden picks. Place rolls on greased baking sheet with sides (see Note).

Spray rolls with cooking spray. Sprinkle with paprika. Bake in 350°F (175°C) oven for about 15 minutes until crisp and golden. Makes 6 rolls.

1 roll: 415 Calories; 6.9 g Total Fat (1.8 g Mono, 0.5 g Poly, 2.8 g Sat); 18 mg Cholesterol; 76 g Carbohydrate; 16 g Fibre; 18 g Protein; 473 mg Sodium

Pictured on page 126.

Note: These rolls freeze well for a quick and convenient snack. Bake from frozen, covered, in 350°F (175°C) oven for 20 minutes. Bake, uncovered, for another 15 minutes until crisp and heated through.

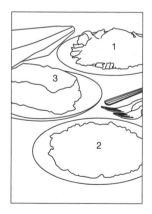

1. Shrimp Rice Skillet, page 98
2. Cajun Chicken and Barley, page 91
3. Lamb Moussaka, page 114

Props courtesy of: Pier 1 Imports
Stokes
Pfaltzgraff Canada

Chocolate Cravings

The devil on your shoulder tempting you with visions of brownies? Here's
an almost-guilt-free square designed with the chocolate lover in mind.
They're even gluten-free!

Canola oil	1/4 cup	60 mL
Unsweetened chocolate baking squares (1 oz., 28 g, each), chopped	4	4
Large eggs, fork-beaten	2	2
Unsweetened applesauce	1/2 cup	125 mL
Granulated sugar	1 cup	250 mL
Vanilla extract	1/2 tsp.	2 mL
Salt	1/8 tsp.	0.5 mL
Brown rice flour	3/4 cup	175 mL
Semi-sweet chocolate chips (optional)	1/2 cup	125 mL
Ground flaxseed (see Tip, page 49)	2 tbsp.	30 mL

Heat canola oil and chocolate in large heavy saucepan on lowest heat for about 10 minutes, stirring often, until chocolate is almost melted. Do not overheat. Remove from heat. Stir until smooth.

Add eggs and applesauce. Mix well.

Add next 3 ingredients. Stir.

Add remaining 3 ingredients. Stir. Spread evenly in greased 8 x 8 inch (20 x 20 cm) baking dish. Bake, uncovered, in 350°F (175°C) oven for about 30 minutes until wooden pick inserted in centre comes out moist but not wet with batter. Do not over bake. Cuts into 25 squares.

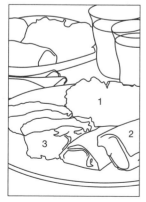

1 square: 101 Calories; 5.4 g Total Fat (2.3 g Mono, 0.8 g Poly, 1.8 g Sat); 15 mg Cholesterol; 13 g Carbohydrate; 1 g Fibre; 1 g Protein; 16 mg Sodium

Pictured on page 144.

1. Chicken Couscous Cakes, page 95
2. Barley Bean Rolls, page 124
3. Italian Rice Cups, page 96

Props courtesy of: Stokes

Coconut Custard Pie

In the battle to eat more whole grains but still satisfy your sweet tooth, consider this custard's last stand. There won't be a slice left after the dessert bell has rung.

CRUST

Barley flour	1 1/2 cups	375 mL
Brown sugar, packed	1 tbsp.	15 mL
Baking powder	1 tsp.	5 mL
Salt	1/4 tsp.	1 mL
Cold butter (or hard margarine), cut up	1/3 cup	75 mL
Ice water	1/3 cup	75 mL

FILLING

Milk	2 cups	500 mL
Coconut extract	1 1/2 tsp.	7 mL
Brown sugar, packed	1/2 cup	125 mL
Barley flour	1/3 cup	75 mL
All-purpose flour	2 tbsp.	30 mL
Salt	1/4 tsp.	1 mL
Milk	3/4 cup	175 mL
Large egg, fork-beaten	1	1
Medium unsweetened coconut, toasted (see Tip, page 28)	1/2 cup	125 mL
Medium unsweetened coconut, toasted (see Tip, page 28)	1/2 cup	125 mL

Crust: Combine first 4 ingredients in medium bowl. Cut in butter until mixture resembles coarse crumbs.

Add ice water, 1 tbsp. (15 mL) at a time, stirring with fork until mixture starts to come together. Do not over mix. Turn out pastry onto work surface. Shape into slightly flattened disc. Wrap with plastic wrap. Chill for 30 minutes. Roll out pastry between 2 sheets of waxed paper to 12 inch (30 cm) diameter circle. Carefully transfer to 9 inch (22 cm) pie plate. Roll under and crimp decorative edge. Bake in 425°F (220°C) oven for about 15 minutes until starting to brown. Let stand on wire rack until cool.

Filling: Combine first amount of milk and extract in medium saucepan. Heat on medium-high for about 3 minutes, stirring occasionally, until hot but not boiling. Remove from heat.

(continued on next page)

Desserts

Combine next 4 ingredients in small bowl. Add second amount of milk and egg. Stir with whisk until combined. Add to hot milk mixture, stirring constantly. Heat and stir on medium until boiling and thickened.

Add first amount of coconut. Stir. Pour into crust.

Sprinkle with second amount of coconut. Cool at room temperature for 10 minutes. Chill for at least 3 hours until set. Cuts into 8 wedges.

1 wedge: 353 Calories; 15.2 g Total Fat (2.7 g Mono, 0.7 g Poly, 10.7 g Sat); 46 mg Cholesterol; 48 g Carbohydrate; 5 g Fibre; 8 g Protein; 290 mg Sodium

Almond Amaranth Cake

Talk about decadent! This dense, lemony dessert is fit for royalty when served warm with a drizzle of honey.

Large eggs (see Note)	7	7
Granulated sugar	1 3/4 cups	425 mL
Lemon juice	1 tbsp.	15 mL
Grated lemon zest	2 tsp.	10 mL
Salt	1/8 tsp.	0.5 mL
Cooked amaranth (see Tip, page 33)	1 cup	250 mL
All-purpose flour	1 cup	250 mL
Ground almonds	1 cup	250 mL
Icing (confectioner's) sugar, sprinkle (optional)		

Beat first 5 ingredients in large bowl until frothy.

Add amaranth. Beat until smooth.

Combine flour and almonds in medium bowl. Fold flour mixture into egg mixture. Pour batter into greased 9 inch (22 cm) springform pan. Bake in 350°F (175°C) oven for about 65 minutes until firm and wooden pick inserted in centre comes out clean. Let stand in pan for 5 minutes. Remove cake from pan and place on wire rack to cool.

Sprinkle with icing sugar. Cuts into 16 wedges.

1 wedge: 222 Calories; 6.0 g Total Fat (3.0 g Mono, 1.4 g Poly, 1.1 g Sat); 81 mg Cholesterol; 37 g Carbohydrate; 3 g Fibre; 7 g Protein; 44 mg Sodium

Note: If cholesterol is a concern, use egg product instead. Substitute each egg with 3 tbsp. (50 mL) egg product.

Wild Rice Upside-Down Cake

Turn this classic dessert upside down in more ways than one! The flavour and texture of wild rice will have you looking at this pineapple-topped (or is it "bottomed"?) cake from a whole new angle!

Brown sugar, packed	2/3 cup	150 mL
Dark (navy) rum	1/4 cup	60 mL
Butter (or hard margarine), softened	2 tbsp.	30 mL
Canned pineapple slices	9	9
Maraschino cherries	9	9
All-purpose flour	3/4 cup	175 mL
Whole-wheat flour	3/4 cup	175 mL
Baking powder	1 1/2 tsp.	7 mL
Baking soda	1 tsp.	5 mL
Salt	1/2 tsp.	2 mL
Large eggs, fork-beaten	2	2
Cooked wild rice (see page 12)	1 1/2 cups	375 mL
Buttermilk (or soured milk, see Tip, page 38)	1 cup	250 mL
Granulated sugar	1 cup	250 mL
Canola oil	1/3 cup	75 mL
Vanilla extract	1 tsp.	5 mL

Combine first 3 ingredients in ungreased 9 x 9 inch (22 x 22 cm) pan. Bake, uncovered, in 350°F (175°C) oven for about 5 minutes until brown sugar is melted and mixture is bubbling. Stir.

Arrange pineapple slices in single layer over brown sugar mixture. Place 1 cherry in centre of each pineapple slice. Place pan on baking sheet. Set aside.

Measure next 5 ingredients into large bowl. Stir. Make a well in centre.

Combine remaining 6 ingredients in medium bowl. Add to well. Stir until just moistened. Carefully pour over pineapple slices. Spread evenly. Pan will be very full. Bake for about 45 minutes until wooden pick inserted in centre comes out clean. Let stand in pan for 5 minutes. Invert onto large serving plate. Cuts into 9 pieces.

1 piece: 429 Calories; 11.9 g Total Fat (5.8 g Mono, 2.7 g Poly, 2.7 g Sat); 49 mg Cholesterol; 74 g Carbohydrate; 3 g Fibre; 6 g Protein; 387 mg Sodium

Whole-Grain Fruit Cobbler

Give this old standby a flavour reformation by adding a whole-grain cereal blend to the works. Not too sweet—but sweet enough to keep everyone smiling.

Brown sugar, packed	1/2 cup	125 mL
All-purpose flour	2 tbsp.	30 mL
Cans of sliced peaches, drained	3	3
(14 oz., 398 mL, each)		
Fresh (or frozen) blueberries	3 cups	750 mL
Cooked hard red wheat (see Tip, page 33)	1 cup	250 mL
Whole-Grain Cereal Blend, page 15	1/2 cup	125 mL
Whole-wheat flour	3/4 cup	175 mL
Granulated sugar	3 tbsp.	50 mL
Baking powder	1 tbsp.	15 mL
Salt	1/4 tsp.	1 mL
Cold butter (or hard margarine), cut up	1/3 cup	75 mL
Large egg, fork-beaten	1	1
Buttermilk (or soured milk, see Tip, page 38)	2/3 cup	150 mL

Combine brown sugar and flour in ungreased 3 quart (3 L) casserole. Add next 3 ingredients. Stir well. Bake, covered, in 400°F (205°C) oven for 30 minutes.

Combine next 5 ingredients in large bowl. Cut in butter until mixture resembles coarse crumbs. Make a well in centre.

Add egg and buttermilk to well. Stir until just moistened. Drop batter by tablespoonfuls over hot fruit mixture. Bake, uncovered, in 375°F (190°C) oven for about 30 minutes until golden and wooden pick inserted in centre of biscuit topping comes out clean. Serves 6.

1 serving: 619 Calories; 12.7 g Total Fat (3.2 g Mono, 1.2 g Poly, 6.7 g Sat); 57 mg Cholesterol; 121 g Carbohydrate; 13 g Fibre; 13 g Protein; 359 mg Sodium

 tip When a recipe calls for grated lemon zest and juice, it's easier to grate the lemon first, then juice it. Be careful not to grate down to the pith (white part of the peel), which is bitter and best avoided.

Blueberry Orange Shortcakes

Short in stature but tall on taste! You can serve these biscuits on their own or shortcake style with blueberries and cream sandwiched in between. (And the blueberry sauce can be used as a topping for waffles or ice cream, too!)

BLUEBERRY ORANGE SAUCE

Fresh (or frozen) blueberries	3 cups	750 mL
Orange juice	1/3 cup	75 mL
Granulated sugar	1/4 cup	60 mL
Cornstarch	1 tbsp.	15 mL
Grated orange zest (see Tip, page 131)	2 tsp.	10 mL
Ground cinnamon, just a pinch		
Butter (or hard margarine)	1 tbsp.	15 mL
Vanilla extract	1 tsp.	5 mL

OAT WHEAT BISCUITS

All-purpose flour	1 cup	250 mL
Large flake rolled oats	1/2 cup	125 mL
Whole-wheat flour	1/2 cup	125 mL
Granulated sugar	1/4 cup	60 mL
Baking powder	2 tsp.	10 mL
Baking soda	1/2 tsp.	2 mL
Salt	1/2 tsp.	2 mL
Cold butter (or hard margarine), cut up	1/3 cup	75 mL
Large egg, fork-beaten	1	1
Buttermilk (or soured milk, see Tip, page 38)	3/4 cup	175 mL
Grated orange zest (see Tip, page 131)	2 tsp.	10 mL
Vanilla extract	2 tsp.	10 mL
Granulated sugar	1 tsp.	5 mL
Frozen light whipped topping, thawed	2 cups	500 mL

Blueberry Orange Sauce: Combine first 6 ingredients in small saucepan. Bring to a boil on medium. Reduce heat to medium-low. Simmer, uncovered, for about 2 minutes, stirring often, until blueberries are softened. Remove from heat.

Add butter and vanilla. Stir. Makes about 2 1/2 cups (625 mL) sauce.

(continued on next page)

132   Desserts

Oat Wheat Biscuits: Combine first 7 ingredients in large bowl. Cut in butter until mixture resembles coarse crumbs. Make a well in centre.

Combine next 4 ingredients in small bowl. Add to well. Stir until just moistened. Drop, using 1/3 cup (75 mL) for each, about 2 inches (5 cm) apart onto greased baking sheet.

Sprinkle sugar over top. Bake in 400°F (205°C) oven for about 15 minutes until golden brown. Let stand on baking sheet for 5 minutes. Remove biscuits from baking sheet and place on wire rack to cool. Cut biscuits in half horizontally. Arrange bottom halves on serving plates. Spoon about 1/4 cup (60 mL) Blueberry Orange Sauce over bottom halves.

Spoon whipped topping over sauce. Place top halves of biscuits over topping. Drizzle remaining sauce over top. Makes 6 shortcakes.

1 shortcake: 624 Calories; 38.4 g Total Fat (10.9 g Mono, 1.7 g Poly, 23.3 g Sat); 151 mg Cholesterol; 63 g Carbohydrate; 5 g Fibre; 9 g Protein; 544 mg Sodium

---

Paré Pointer

He was the teacher's pet because she couldn't afford a dog.

Chili Fruit Tarts

Sweet fruit filling gets a kick of flavour from a spicy-sweet chili sauce.

FILLING

Apple juice	1/3 cup	75 mL
Coarsely chopped dried cherries	1/3 cup	75 mL
Cracked wheat	1/4 cup	60 mL
Ground cinnamon	1/8 tsp.	0.5 mL
Chopped peeled cooking apple (such as McIntosh)	1 1/3 cups	325 mL
Brown sugar, packed	1/4 cup	60 mL
Sweet chili sauce	2 tbsp.	30 mL
All-purpose flour	1 tbsp.	15 mL
Lime juice	2 tsp.	10 mL

PASTRY

Whole-wheat flour	1 1/2 cups	375 mL
Granulated sugar	1 tbsp.	15 mL
Cold butter (or hard margarine), cut up	1/2 cup	125 mL
Ice water	1/3 cup	75 mL
Large egg	1	1
Water	1 tbsp.	15 mL

Filling: Pour apple juice into small saucepan. Bring to a boil. Remove from heat. Add next 3 ingredients. Stir. Let stand, covered, for 5 minutes.

Add next 5 ingredients. Stir.

Pastry: Combine flour and granulated sugar in medium bowl. Cut in butter until mixture resembles coarse crumbs.

Add ice water, 1 tbsp. (15 mL) at a time, stirring with fork until mixture starts to come together. Do not over mix. Turn out pastry onto work surface. Shape into slightly flattened square. Wrap with plastic wrap. Chill for 30 minutes. Roll out pastry on lightly floured surface to 12 x 16 inch (30 x 40 cm) rectangle, about 1/8 inch (3 mm) thick. Cut into twelve 4 inch (10 cm) squares. Press squares into bottom and sides of 12 greased muffin cups. Spoon about 2 tbsp. (30 mL) filling into each cup. Fold corners of pastry over filling.

(continued on next page)

Desserts

Whisk egg and water in separate small bowl. Brush tarts with egg mixture. Bake in 375°F (190°C) oven for about 30 minutes until golden brown. Let stand in pan for 5 minutes. Remove tarts from pan and place on wire rack to cool. Makes 12 tarts.

1 tart: 184 Calories; 8.3 g Total Fat (2.2 g Mono, 0.5 g Poly, 5.0 g Sat); 36 mg Cholesterol; 25 g Carbohydrate; 3 g Fibre; 3 g Protein; 100 mg Sodium

Pictured on page 143.

Brown Rice Pudding

This cranberry and orange-flavoured delight belongs to the best-known category of comfort food—comfort dessert! It's also comforting to know you're getting a good portion of whole grains.

Large eggs	3	3
Granulated sugar	1/3 cup	75 mL
Milk	2 cups	500 mL
Cooked long-grain brown rice (see page 10)	1 1/2 cups	375 mL
Butter (or hard margarine), melted	1 tbsp.	15 mL
Vanilla extract	1 1/2 tsp.	7 mL
Grated orange zest	1 tsp.	5 mL
Salt	1/2 tsp.	2 mL
Ground cinnamon	1/8 tsp.	0.5 mL
Dried cranberries	1/2 cup	125 mL
Slivered almonds, toasted (see Tip, page 28)	1/2 cup	125 mL

Whisk eggs and sugar in medium bowl until sugar is dissolved and mixture is frothy. Add next 7 ingredients. Stir. Transfer to greased 2 quart (2 L) shallow baking dish. Place baking dish in large pan (see Note). Carefully pour boiling water into pan until water comes halfway up sides of baking dish. Bake, uncovered, in 325°F (160°C) oven for 30 minutes. Stir. Bake for another 20 minutes until set.

Sprinkle with cranberries and almonds. Serves 6.

1 serving: 267 Calories; 10.4 g Total Fat (4.9 g Mono, 1.8 g Poly, 2.9 g Sat); 101 mg Cholesterol; 36 g Carbohydrate; 3 g Fibre; 9 g Protein; 282 mg Sodium

Note: Make sure that your baking dish fits into the baking pan before you start. If you don't have a large enough pan, a large roasting pan will also work.

Amaranth Baklava

A test-kitchen favourite, this baklava got rave reviews not only for its fantastic flavours but for its health-conscious approach—we reduced the fat by substituting grains for nuts. Remember to let set overnight.

Granulated sugar	3 cups	750 mL
Water	2 cups	500 mL
Medium lemon, cut into 1/4 inch (6 mm) slices, end slices discarded	1	1
Cooked amaranth (see page 9)	2 cups	500 mL
Coarsely chopped unsalted mixed nuts	1 1/2 cups	375 mL
Granulated sugar	2 tbsp.	30 mL
Ground cinnamon	1 tsp.	5 mL
Ground cloves	1/8 tsp.	0.5 mL
Phyllo pastry sheets, thawed according to package directions	14	14
Butter, melted	3/4 cup	175 mL

Combine first 3 ingredients in medium saucepan. Heat and stir on medium for about 2 minutes until sugar is dissolved. Increase heat to medium-high. Brush side of saucepan with wet pastry brush to dissolve any sugar crystals. Boil for 12 minutes, without stirring. Remove from heat. Discard lemon slices.

Combine next 5 ingredients in medium bowl. Add 1/2 cup (125 mL) lemon mixture. Mix well.

Lay 1 pastry sheet on work surface, with longest side closest to you. Keep remaining sheets covered with damp towel to prevent drying. Brush sheet with melted butter. Fold in half crosswise. Place in greased 9 x 13 inch (22 x 33 cm) pan. Brush with melted butter. Repeat with 4 more pastry sheets and melted butter. Spread half of amaranth mixture over pastry. Repeat layering with another 4 folded sheets of pastry over amaranth mixture, brushing with melted butter after each layer. Spread remaining amaranth mixture over top. Repeat layering with remaining pastry sheets, brushing with remaining melted butter after each layer. To score diamond pattern across pastry using a sharp knife, insert knife down into pastry, almost, but not quite through, to bottom of pan. Make 5 cuts lengthwise, about 1 1/2 inches (3.8 cm) apart. Cut at an angle across lengthwise cuts to make diamond shapes (see diagram).

(continued on next page)

Bake in 350°F (175°C) oven for about 40 minutes until deep golden brown and crisp. Keep hot. Heat remaining lemon mixture until hot. Slowly pour over hot pastry, allowing it to fill spaces and score marks. Let stand, uncovered, at room temperature for at least 6 hours or overnight. Cut through to bottom, following scored diamond pattern. Makes about 30 diamond-shaped pieces.

1 piece: 234 Calories; 9.5 g Total Fat (3.8 g Mono, 1.4 g Poly, 3.7 g Sat); 12 mg Cholesterol; 35 g Carbohydrate; 3 g Fibre; 4 g Protein; 79 mg Sodium

Pictured on page 143.

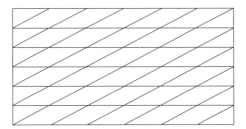

Quinoa Apple Carrot Cake

"Carrot" all for a healthier version of this beloved cake? It looks like your ordinary carrot cake, but quinoa and apple add an appealing dimension of taste.

All-purpose flour	1 1/2 cups	375 mL
Baking powder	1 tsp.	5 mL
Ground cinnamon	1 tsp.	5 mL
Baking soda	1/2 tsp.	2 mL
Salt	1/2 tsp.	2 mL
Large eggs, fork-beaten	3	3
Brown sugar, packed	1 cup	250 mL
Canola oil	2/3 cup	150 mL
Finely grated ginger root (or 3/4 tsp., 4 mL, ground ginger)	1 tbsp.	15 mL
Cooked quinoa (see page 11)	1 1/2 cups	375 mL
Grated carrot	1 cup	250 mL
Grated peeled cooking apple (such as McIntosh)	1/2 cup	125 mL
ICING		
Cream cheese, softened	2 tbsp.	30 mL
Milk	2 tbsp.	30 mL
Butter (or hard margarine), softened	2 tsp.	10 mL
Vanilla extract	1/4 tsp.	1 mL
Icing (confectioner's) sugar	1 1/2 cups	375 mL

Measure first 5 ingredients into large bowl. Stir. Make a well in centre.

Combine next 4 ingredients in medium bowl.

Add next 3 ingredients. Stir. Add to well. Stir until just moistened. Line bottom of greased 9 inch (22 cm) springform pan with waxed paper. Spread batter evenly in pan. Bake in 325°F (160°C) oven for about 55 minutes until wooden pick inserted in centre comes out clean. Run knife around inside edge of pan to loosen cake. Let stand in pan for 5 minutes. Invert cake onto wire rack to cool completely. Remove and discard waxed paper from bottom of cake.

(continued on next page)

Desserts

Icing: Beat first 4 ingredients in small bowl until smooth.

Add icing sugar. Beat until smooth. Add more milk if necessary until spreading consistency. Spread evenly over top and side of cooled cake. Cuts into 12 wedges.

1 wedge: 406 Calories; 15.7 g Total Fat (8.1 g Mono, 4.2 g Poly, 2.3 g Sat); 51 mg Cholesterol; 61 g Carbohydrate; 2 g Fibre; 6 g Protein; 218 mg Sodium

Pictured on page 143.

Paré Pointer

Of course the president wore the largest hat.
He had the biggest head.

Steamed Maple Plum Cake

Keep Little Jack Horner in the corner and away from this scrumptious cake.
Although there's plenty of plums to go around, we consider his habit of fishing
for plums with his thumbs to be bad manners!

Whole-wheat flour	1 3/4 cups	425 mL
All-purpose flour	1/2 cup	125 mL
Baking powder	1 tbsp.	15 mL
Butter (or hard margarine), softened	1/2 cup	125 mL
Brown sugar, packed	1 cup	250 mL
Large eggs	3	3
Cooked amaranth (see page 9)	1/2 cup	125 mL
Maple (or maple-flavoured) syrup	2 tbsp.	30 mL
Vanilla extract	1/2 tsp.	2 mL
Fresh black plums, peeled, pitted and sliced	3	3
Maple (or maple-flavoured) syrup	1/3 cup	75 mL

Combine first 3 ingredients in small bowl.

Cream butter and sugar in medium bowl. Add eggs 1 at a time, beating well after each addition. Add next 3 ingredients. Beat until smooth. Add flour mixture. Stir until blended. Spread evenly in greased 9 x 9 inch (22 x 22 cm) baking dish.

Arrange plum slices over batter, pressing down lightly. Pour second amount of maple syrup over top. Cover with greased foil. Place baking dish on wire rack set in large roasting pan. Carefully pour hot water into roasting pan until water comes halfway up sides of baking dish. Bake, covered, in 350°F (175°C) oven for about 60 minutes until cake springs back when gently pressed. Remove from roasting pan. Let stand on wire rack for 5 minutes. Cuts into 16 pieces.

1 piece: 229 Calories; 7.3 g Total Fat (2.0 g Mono, 0.7 g Poly, 4.0 g Sat); 50 mg Cholesterol; 38 g Carbohydrate; 3 g Fibre; 4 g Protein; 109 mg Sodium

Pictured on page 143.

UPSIDE-DOWN PLUM CAKE: Pour second amount of maple syrup into bottom of greased baking dish. Arrange plum slices over top. Carefully pour batter over plum slices. Spread evenly. Bake as directed. Invert onto large serving plate.

Munch 'n' Crunch Mix

Whether you're on the trail or just taking a break at work, this snack mix is an excellent choice!

Large flake rolled oats	2 cups	500 mL
Whole natural almonds	1 cup	250 mL
Raw pumpkin seeds	1/2 cup	125 mL
Raw sunflower seeds	1/2 cup	125 mL
Whole buckwheat	1/2 cup	125 mL
Honey	1/3 cup	75 mL
Canola oil	3 tbsp.	50 mL
Brown sugar, packed	2 tbsp.	30 mL
Ground cinnamon	1 tsp.	5 mL
Vanilla extract	1 tsp.	5 mL
Popped corn (about 4 tsp., 20 mL, unpopped)	2 cups	500 mL
Chopped dried pineapple	1/2 cup	125 mL
Dried cranberries	1/4 cup	60 mL
Raisins	1/4 cup	60 mL

Combine first 5 ingredients in large bowl.

Combine next 5 ingredients in small saucepan. Heat and stir on medium until brown sugar is dissolved. Drizzle over oat mixture. Stir until coated. Spread evenly on 2 ungreased baking sheets with sides. Bake on separate racks in 300°F (150°C) oven for about 20 minutes, switching position at halftime, until golden. Transfer to same large bowl.

Add popped corn. Toss.

Add remaining 3 ingredients. Toss until coated. Makes about 8 cups (2 L).

1 cup (250 mL): 487 Calories; 24.1 g Total Fat (9.2 g Mono, 4.4 g Poly, 2.8 g Sat); 0 mg Cholesterol; 57 g Carbohydrate; 7 g Fibre; 13 g Protein; 11 mg Sodium

Whole-Grain Snack Cake

Longing for chocolate? You don't have to refrain. Try this moist snack cake that's full of whole grain.

All-purpose flour	1 1/4 cups	300 mL
Brown sugar, packed	3/4 cup	175 mL
Whole-Grain Cereal Blend, page 15	3/4 cup	175 mL
Baking powder	1 tsp.	5 mL
Baking soda	1 tsp.	5 mL
Salt	1/2 tsp.	2 mL
Large eggs, fork-beaten	2	2
Mashed overripe banana	1 1/2 cups	375 mL
Buttermilk (or soured milk, see Tip, page 38)	1 cup	250 mL
Mini semi-sweet chocolate chips	1/2 cup	125 mL
Canola oil	1/4 cup	60 mL
Vanilla extract	1 tsp.	5 mL

Measure first 6 ingredients into large bowl. Stir. Make a well in centre.

Combine remaining 6 ingredients in medium bowl. Add to well. Stir until just moistened. Spread in greased 9 x 13 inch (22 x 33 cm) pan. Bake in 375°F (190°C) oven for about 40 minutes until wooden pick inserted in centre comes out clean. Let stand in pan to cool completely. Cuts into 12 squares.

1 square: 263 Calories; 8.3 g Total Fat (3.9 g Mono, 1.8 g Poly, 2.1 g Sat); 32 mg Cholesterol; 44 g Carbohydrate; 2 g Fibre; 5 g Protein; 264 mg Sodium

1. Amaranth Baklava, page 136
2. Steamed Maple Plum Cake, page 140
3. Chili Fruit Tarts, page 134
4. Quinoa Apple Carrot Cake, page 138

Props courtesy of: Winners Stores
Casa Bugatti
Danesco Inc.

Puffed Wheat Fruit Squares

Crunchy, chewy, buttery and sweet, these puffed wheat squares can't be beat—especially since we added apples and cranberries!

Puffed wheat cereal	6 cups	1.5 L
Sliced natural almonds, toasted (see Tip, page 28)	3/4 cup	175 mL
Diced dried apple	2/3 cup	150 mL
Dried cranberries	2/3 cup	150 mL
Brown sugar, packed	1 cup	250 mL
Corn syrup	1/2 cup	125 mL
Butter (or hard margarine)	1/3 cup	75 mL
Peanut butter	2 tbsp.	30 mL
Whole buckwheat, toasted (see Tip, page 31)	1 cup	250 mL
Vanilla extract	1 tsp.	5 mL

Combine first 4 ingredients in large bowl. Set aside.

Combine next 4 ingredients in medium saucepan. Heat and stir on medium until sugar is dissolved and mixture starts to boil. Boil for 1 minute. Remove from heat.

Add buckwheat and vanilla. Stir for 1 minute. Pour over puffed wheat mixture. Stir until coated. Press evenly into greased 9 x 13 inch (22 x 33 cm) pan. Cool at room temperature until firm. Cuts into 24 squares.

1 square: 152 Calories; 4.9 g Total Fat (2.0 g Mono, 0.8 g Poly, 1.8 g Sat); 6 mg Cholesterol; 27 g Carbohydrate; 2 g Fibre; 2 g Protein; 63 mg Sodium

Pictured at left.

1. Puffed Wheat Fruit Squares, above
2. Chocolate Peanut Cookies, page 147
3. Seeds 'n' Grains, page 146
4. Chocolate Cravings, page 127

Props courtesy of: Winners Stores

Seeds 'n' Grains

Do you crave those supermarket sesame snacks? Well, it's a snap to make them at home.

Granulated sugar	1 cup	250 mL
Water	1/4 cup	60 mL
White corn syrup	1/4 cup	60 mL
Amaranth, toasted (see Tip, page 31)	1/4 cup	60 mL
Quinoa (see Note 1), toasted (see Tip, page 31)	1/4 cup	60 mL
Sesame seeds, toasted (see Tip, page 28)	1/4 cup	60 mL
Salt	1/4 tsp.	1 mL

Place baking sheet with sides upside down on work surface. Place sheet of parchment (not waxed) paper on bottom of baking sheet. Cut another piece of parchment (not waxed) paper the same size. Set aside. Combine first 3 ingredients in medium heavy saucepan. Heat and stir on medium until sugar is dissolved and mixture starts to boil. Brush side of saucepan with wet pastry brush to dissolve any sugar crystals. Boil for about 15 minutes, without stirring, until hard crack stage (300° to 310°F, 150° to 154°C) on candy thermometer (see Tip, page 148) or until small amount dropped into very cold water separates into hard, brittle threads. Remove from heat.

Add remaining 4 ingredients. Mix well. Pour lengthwise along centre of parchment paper. Place second sheet of parchment paper on top. Working quickly, use rolling pin to press grain mixture to about 1/16 inch (1.5 mm) thickness. Be careful not to squeeze hot sugar mixture out sides of parchment paper. Let stand for 2 minutes. Remove top sheet of parchment paper. Let stand until starting to firm. Cut into 1 x 2 inch (2.5 x 5 cm) rectangles (see Note 2). Makes 13 oz. (370 g), about 38 pieces.

1 oz. (28 g): 106 Calories; 1.6 g Total Fat (0.6 g Mono, 0.7 g Poly, 0.3 g Sat); 0 mg Cholesterol; 23 g Carbohydrate; 1 g Fibre; 1 g Protein; 50 mg Sodium

Pictured on page 144.

Note 1: Do not rinse quinoa before toasting.

Note 2: It is easiest to cut the mixture while it is still a little warm.

Chocolate Peanut Cookies

Peanut, peanut butter! Our take on classic peanut butter cookies uses applesauce,
banana and, the piéce de résistance, chocolate!

Butter (or hard margarine), softened	1/4 cup	60 mL
Brown sugar, packed	2/3 cup	150 mL
Peanut butter	1/2 cup	125 mL
Large eggs	2	2
Mashed overripe banana	1/2 cup	125 mL
Unsweetened applesauce	1/3 cup	75 mL
Vanilla extract	1 tsp.	5 mL
Large flake rolled oats	1 cup	250 mL
All-purpose flour	2/3 cup	150 mL
Whole-wheat flour	2/3 cup	150 mL
Cocoa, sifted if lumpy	1/2 cup	125 mL
Baking soda	1/2 tsp.	2 mL
Salt	1/2 tsp.	2 mL
Mini semi-sweet chocolate chips	1/2 cup	125 mL
Chopped salted peanuts	1/3 cup	75 mL

Cream first 3 ingredients in large bowl. Add next 4 ingredients. Beat well.

Combine next 6 ingredients in medium bowl. Add to butter mixture in 2 additions, mixing well after each addition until no dry flour remains.

Add chocolate chips and peanuts. Mix well. Roll dough into 1 1/2 inch (3.8 cm) balls. Arrange balls about 2 inches (5 cm) apart on greased cookie sheets. Bake in 350°F (175°C) oven for 8 to 10 minutes until firm and golden. Let stand on cookie sheets for 5 minutes. Remove cookies from cookie sheets and place on wire racks to cool. Makes about 40 cookies.

1 cookie: 88 Calories; 4.2 g Total Fat (1.3 g Mono, 0.6 g Poly, 1.8 g Sat); 12 mg Cholesterol;
12 g Carbohydrate; 1 g Fibre; 2 g Protein; 59 mg Sodium

Pictured on page 144.

Almond Buckwheat Brittle

A sweet brittle with a buttery, almond flavour. Toasted buckwheat adds crunch—without the fat and calories of nuts.

Granulated sugar	3/4 cup	175 mL
White corn syrup	1/2 cup	125 mL
Water	1/4 cup	60 mL
Salt	1/8 tsp.	0.5 mL
Butter (or hard margarine)	1 tbsp.	15 mL
Almond extract	1/2 tsp.	2 mL
Baking soda	1/2 tsp.	2 mL
Whole buckwheat, toasted (see Tip, page 31)	1 1/2 cups	375 mL

Combine first 4 ingredients in small heavy saucepan. Heat and stir on medium until sugar is dissolved and mixture starts to boil. Brush side of saucepan with wet pastry brush to dissolve any sugar crystals. Boil for about 15 minutes, without stirring, until hard-crack stage (300° to 310°F, 150° to 154°C) on candy thermometer (see Tip, below) or until small amount dropped into very cold water separates into hard, brittle threads. Remove from heat.

Add next 3 ingredients. Stir. Add buckwheat. Mix well. Immediately turn out onto 10 inch (25 cm) sheet of parchment (not waxed) paper. Place another sheet of parchment (not waxed) paper on top. Working quickly, use rolling pin to press buckwheat mixture into 8 x 10 inch (20 x 25 cm) rectangle. Let stand for about 30 minutes until completely cooled. Break brittle into small pieces. Store in tightly covered container. Makes 1 lb. (454 g), about 24 pieces.

1 oz. (28 g): 97 Calories; 1.0 g Total Fat (0.3 g Mono, 0.1 g Poly, 0.5 g Sat); 2 mg Cholesterol; 22 g Carbohydrate; 1 g Fibre; 1 g Protein; 65 mg Sodium

 tip Test your candy thermometer before each use. Bring water to a boil. Candy thermometer should read 212°F (100°C) at sea level. Adjust recipe temperature up or down based on test results. For example, if your thermometer reads 206°F (97°C), subtract 6°F (3°C) from each temperature called for in the recipe.

Almond Oat Popcorn Squares

How many popcorn balls can you stuff into your pocket without looking a bit bumpy?
Thin, yet chewy and satisfying, these popcorn squares will slide into your pocket
virtually unnoticed!

Popped corn (about 1/3 cup, 75 mL, unpopped)	8 cups	2 L
Large flake rolled oats	2 cups	500 mL
Chopped pitted dates	1 cup	250 mL
Chopped whole natural almonds, toasted (see Tip, page 28)	1 cup	250 mL
Brown sugar, packed	1/2 cup	125 mL
Honey	1/2 cup	125 mL

Spread popcorn in greased 9 x 13 inch (22 x 33 cm) pan. Sprinkle next 3 ingredients over popcorn.

Combine brown sugar and honey in small saucepan. Bring to a boil on medium. Pour over popcorn mixture. Toss gently. Bake in 300°F (150°C) oven for 10 minutes. Stir. Bake for another 10 minutes. Remove from oven. Stir well. Pack down lightly in even layer. Let stand for 15 minutes. Cuts into 12 squares (see Note).

1 square: 271 Calories; 7.2 g Total Fat (4.1 g Mono, 1.9 g Poly, 0.7 g Sat); 0 mg Cholesterol; 48 g Carbohydrate; 5 g Fibre; 6 g Protein; 6 mg Sodium

Note: It is easiest to cut the squares while they are still a little warm.

Measurement Tables

Throughout this book measurements are given in Conventional and Metric measure. To compensate for differences between the two measurements due to rounding, a full metric measure is not always used. The cup used is the standard 8 fluid ounce. Temperature is given in degrees Fahrenheit and Celsius. Baking pan measurements are in inches and centimetres as well as quarts and litres. An exact metric conversion is given below as well as the working equivalent (Metric Standard Measure).

Spoons

Conventional Measure	Metric Exact Conversion Millilitre (mL)	Metric Standard Measure Millilitre (mL)
1/8 teaspoon (tsp.)	0.6 mL	0.5 mL
1/4 teaspoon (tsp.)	1.2 mL	1 mL
1/2 teaspoon (tsp.)	2.4 mL	2 mL
1 teaspoon (tsp.)	4.7 mL	5 mL
2 teaspoons (tsp.)	9.4 mL	10 mL
1 tablespoon (tbsp.)	14.2 mL	15 mL

Cups

Conventional Measure	Metric Exact Conversion Millilitre (mL)	Metric Standard Measure Millilitre (mL)
1/4 cup (4 tbsp.)	56.8 mL	60 mL
1/3 cup (5 1/3 tbsp.)	75.6 mL	75 mL
1/2 cup (8 tbsp.)	113.7 mL	125 mL
2/3 cup (10 2/3 tbsp.)	151.2 mL	150 mL
3/4 cup (12 tbsp.)	170.5 mL	175 mL
1 cup (16 tbsp.)	227.3 mL	250 mL
4 1/2 cups	1022.9 mL	1000 mL (1 L)

Oven Temperatures

Fahrenheit (°F)	Celsius (°C)
175°	80°
200°	95°
225°	110°
250°	120°
275°	140°
300°	150°
325°	160°
350°	175°
375°	190°
400°	205°
425°	220°
450°	230°
475°	240°
500°	260°

Dry Measurements

Conventional Measure Ounces (oz.)	Metric Exact Conversion Grams (g)	Metric Standard Measure Grams (g)
1 oz.	28.3 g	28 g
2 oz.	56.7 g	57 g
3 oz.	85.0 g	85 g
4 oz.	113.4 g	125 g
5 oz.	141.7 g	140 g
6 oz.	170.1 g	170 g
7 oz.	198.4 g	200 g
8 oz.	226.8 g	250 g
16 oz.	453.6 g	500 g
32 oz.	907.2 g	1000 g (1 kg)

Pans

Conventional Inches	Metric Centimetres
8x8 inch	20x20 cm
9x9 inch	22x22 cm
9x13 inch	22x33 cm
10x15 inch	25x38 cm
11x17 inch	28x43 cm
8x2 inch round	20x5 cm
9x2 inch round	22x5 cm
10x4 1/2 inch tube	25x11 cm
8x4x3 inch loaf	20x10x7.5 cm
9x5x3 inch loaf	22x12.5x7.5 cm

Casseroles

CANADA & BRITAIN		UNITED STATES	
Standard Size Casserole	Exact Metric Measure	Standard Size Casserole	Exact Metric Measure
1 qt. (5 cups)	1.13 L	1 qt. (4 cups)	900 mL
1 1/2 qts. (7 1/2 cups)	1.69 L	1 1/2 qts. (6 cups)	1.35 L
2 qts. (10 cups)	2.25 L	2 qts. (8 cups)	1.8 L
2 1/2 qts. (12 1/2 cups)	2.81 L	2 1/2 qts. (10 cups)	2.25 L
3 qts. (15 cups)	3.38 L	3 qts. (12 cups)	2.7 L
4 qts. (20 cups)	4.5 L	4 qts. (16 cups)	3.6 L
5 qts. (25 cups)	5.63 L	5 qts. (20 cups)	4.5 L

Recipe Index

151

153

154

155

Cookies

Sign up to receive our **FREE online newsletter,** and we'll let you know when new cookbooks are available for purchase.

www.companyscoming.com

Cookies
We're now releasing *Cookies* with a new and improved look! You'll still find all the same great recipes that you've come to know and love. The tough part will be deciding which cookie to try fir

Try it

a sample recipe from *Cookies*

Orange Bran Cookies

Cookies, Page 12

A wonderful breakfast cookie.

Butter (or hard margarine), softened	1/2 cup	125 mL
Granulated sugar	1/2 cup	125 mL
Large egg	1	1
Prepared orange juice	2 tbsp.	30 mL
Grated orange rind	1 1/2 tsp.	7 mL
All-purpose flour	1 cup	250 mL
Baking powder	1 tsp.	5 mL
Salt 1/2 tsp.	2 mL	
Bran flakes cereal	1 cup	250 mL
Semisweet chocolate chips (optional)	1 cup	250 mL

Cream butter and sugar together. Beat in egg. Add orange juice and rind.

Add remaining ingredients. Mix well. Drop by spoonfuls onto greased cookie sheet. Bake in 350°F (180°C) oven for 10 to 12 minutes. Makes 3 dozen.

Celebrating the
Harvest
RECIPES FOR FALL & WINTER GATHERINGS

Whether from the garden, farmers' market or supermarket, harvest ingredients display the bounty and beauty of nature. Entertain a crowd in style, or feed your family comfort food they'll not soon forget—with new delicious recipes that celebrate harvest ingredients. What a lovely way to get through the long fall and winter!

SPECIAL OCCASION SERIES

If you like what we've done with **cooking,** you'll **love** what we do with **crafts!**